I OWE MY LIFE . . .

I OWE MY LIFE . . .

COMPILED AND EDITED BY
Pauline Samuelson

FOREWORD BY
H. M. Queen Elizabeth The Queen Mother, Deputy President of the British Red Cross Society

BLOOMSBURY

First published in 1995 by
Bloomsbury Publishing Plc
2 Soho Square
London, W1V 5DE

Picture Acknowledgements
No. 26 by Liliane de Toledo FRCCS, courtesy of International Community
of the Red Cross.
All other photographs courtesy of British Red Cross Museum and Archives.

The moral right of the authors has been asserted

A copy of the CIP entry for this is available from the
British Library

ISBN 0 7475 2020 8

10 9 8 7 6 5 4 3 2 1

Typeset by Hewer Text Composition Services, Edinburgh
Printed in Britain by Clays Ltd, St Ives plc

CONTENTS

THE INTERNATIONAL RED CROSS

I hope that readers of this Anthology will gain an insight into the breadth of Red Cross work undertaken by generations of dedicated volunteers, for so many people only think of the Red Cross as dealing with disasters in overseas countries or in times of war.

The history of the British Red Cross is a story of unstinting service both to the people of this nation and in the cause of world humanity, and I look back with pride on the many years of association I have had with the Society.

Elizabeth R

1994

Editor's Note

MOST OF US TAKE THE RED CROSS for granted. Lockerbie, Sarajevo, Belfast – quietly the Red Cross is always there behind the scenes.

It is 125 years since the British Red Cross Society first began its humanitarian mission by giving aid to both sides in the Franco-Prussian War of 1870. This anthology marks the occasion with a collection of stories that record the history of our National Society as seen through the eyes of those who have first-hand knowledge of its work: the people on the spot and some of those who owe their life to the Red Cross.

The Society is indebted to the contributors for so generously giving their time and energy to tell us their Red Cross tales. I should like to add a personal note of thanks to John Gray, Director, Public Affairs Division at the National Headquarters of the British Red Cross, who conceived the notion of this commemorative publication and whose sustained encouragement and enthusiasm have guaranteed the pleasure I have had in editing this anthology.

The variety of subjects included in this book illustrate the scope of an organisation which is so well known yet so little understood. I hope through these stories that readers will gain a better idea of the service the British Red Cross has given in the cause of humanity through the years 1870 to 1995.

Pauline Samuelson, OBE
British Red Cross National Headquarters, London, 1994

INTRODUCTION

WERE YOU EVER RASH ENOUGH to ask someone in the Red Cross, 'How did it all begin?', you would probably receive a knowing smile and a swift launch into their favourite story – the battle of Solferino and the birth of a great idea.

If the story-teller could be interrupted long enough for another question, 'What were things like before the Red Cross?', that is where this book starts, for it is useful to get a picture of how fighting men were treated before the advent of the Geneva Convention.

All through the history of wars, help of some kind has been given to wounded men on the battlefield. The help varied greatly in quality through the centuries and depended as much on the status of the soldier as where in the world the battle was being waged. During the days of the Roman Empire the Roman army fared exceptionally well. There were hospitals in each legionary fort and a *medicus vulnerum*, doctor of wounds, to treat the wounded close to the battlefield. Of course, no enemy wounded were treated, but the standard of care given to Roman soldiers was not to be equalled again for hundreds of years.

In the Middle Ages monastic orders occasionally sent their members into the battlefield to tend the wounded, giving them sanctuary in the monasteries. During the Crusades, a formal system of evacuation was organised by the Knights Hospitalers, who nursed the sick and wounded in their own hospitals. European armies, however, made very little provision for the wounded in war. By and large only the high-born received treatment for their wounds. At the battle of Agincourt in 1415, for instance, Henry V was attended by a physician, a surgeon and twelve assistants. The common soldier's only hope of help came from an army's camp followers.

With the growth of nation states in the 16th century, governments started to look at ways of limiting the brutalities of war. Agreements were drawn up for specific campaigns, and treaties were made that helped not only the sick and wounded, but also the prisoners of war. To include this last category was a real step forward as it put an end to the ransoming of prisoners. This practice could make a free soldier's fortune, but it could also ruin a prisoner's family. One of the first formal agreements to end this practice came in 1689 when France and Spain agreed to exchange prisoners of war without ransom and to look after them in hospitals if they were wounded.

During the War of Austrian Succession and after the Battle of Dettingen in 1743, a treaty and convention was signed for 'The Sick, Wounded and Prisoners of War of the Auxiliary Troops of His Very Christian Majesty (Louis XV) and Those of the Allies'. This treaty became a basis for the drafting of subsequent conventions.

Yet while these humanitarian acts marked a gradual improvement for victims of war, the number of casualties grew steadily as weaponry and battle techniques became more sophisticated. The conditions in which the sick and the wounded were tended were often deplorable. One great Napoleonic surgeon, Baron Percy, describing the siege of Danzig in 1807, writes of the 1,600 wounded and 2,000 sick 'with not a straw mattress nor a basin nor a nurse between them'. Moreover, lack of transport meant that it was not unusual for the wounded to lie on the battlefield for several days after they had fallen.

In times past, care of the wounded depended on the compassion and interest of individual military leaders. Army surgeons played an important part in developing better and quicker procedures to help the sick and wounded. The armies of Roman Catholic countries were especially fortunate as they benefited from the tradition of nursing nuns.

By contrast, the British Army Medical Service was in poor shape until the formidable Florence Nightingale arrived on the scene during the Crimean War. Not only did her heroic efforts produce great reforms in the condition of military hospitals, but she triumphantly succeeded in changing the status and image of the British nurse forever.

By the outbreak of the Crimean War in 1853, almost a whole generation of Britons had grown up in peace following the Congress of Vienna. Earlier wars, which had seemed remote, were now replaced by a conflict that seemed to be right on the doorstep. Instant news was telegraphed home by the famous war correspondent William Russell of *The Times*, and the first conscripted British Force sent letters back home using the newly formed Postal Union. Soldiers vividly described the tragedy of Scutari to their families, and for the first time the whole nation came to understand the suffering endured by sick and wounded fighting men.

This was the Age of Reform. And this was the moment in history when Henry Dunant, known as the father of the Red Cross, was destined to join that growing band of world reformers to whom humanity will always owe an imperishable debt of gratitude.

THE EARLY
YEARS

THE MAN IN WHITE

Pauline Samuelson

Henry Dunant, founding father of the Red Cross, was born in Geneva in 1828 at a time when Switzerland was overflowing with political refugees fleeing from neighbouring Italy, recently handed over to Austria after the turmoil of the Napoleonic Wars. From his early youth, Dunant was involved with good causes, although at the time that our story begins he was mainly concerned with furthering his own business career. It was with this thought in mind that he planned a journey to northern Italy, where he hoped to have a meeting with Napoleon III. The Emperor, as commander-in-chief of the French forces, was engaged in a war against Austria.

Dunant left Geneva in June 1859, impeccably dressed in a white tropical suit in anticipation of his meeting with the Emperor. On the evening of his arrival in Castiglione – 'the memorable twenty-fourth of June', as he later wrote in his book *Un Souvenir de Solferino* – the armies of France and Sardinia had fought the Austrian forces in a battle to which the village of Solferino gives its name. At the end of a day of fearful fighting, the Austrian Emperor withdrew his forces, pursued by the French and the Sardinians.

The military arrangements for the care of the fallen had collapsed during the battle; even the few ambulances were shelled indiscriminately. Dunant, coming upon the aftermath, described the scene with moving simplicity in his later chronicle: 'Many an officer and soldier went searching high and low for a comrade, countryman or a friend. If he came across someone he knew, he would kneel at his side trying to bring him back to life, press his hand, staunch the bleeding, or bind the broken limb with a handkerchief. But there was no water to be had for the poor sufferers. How many silent tears were shed that miserable night when all false pride, all human decency even, were forgotten.'

For three days and nights Dunant forgot his original reason for travelling to Italy, while he tried to give what help he could to the wounded and dying, who were brought in by farm carts to the small town of Castiglione. He became known as 'the man in white' as he gathered around him willing hands and set about organising a makeshift hospital in the local church. 'Men of all nations lay side by side,' he wrote in his book. 'Frenchmen, Arabs, Germans and Slavs. . . . Oh, the agony and the suffering. . . . But the women of Castiglione, seeing that I made no distinction between nationalities, followed my example, showing kindness to all these men. "Tutti fratelli" – all are brothers – they repeated feelingly.'

Dunant's moving testament, translated into English as *A Memory of Solferino*, was written three years after his haunting experience in Italy. His profound belief in a practical solution to help the victims of future wars led him to write, 'Oh, how valuable it would have been in those Lombardy towns to have had a hundred experienced and qualified voluntary orderlies and nurses!' He went on to propose, 'Would it not be possible in time of peace and quiet to form relief societies for the purpose of having care given to the wounded in war-time by zealous, devoted and thoroughly qualified volunteers?'

The wide circulation of the book, published in 1862, meant that it was read by people of influence all over Europe. Many were deeply affected by its message. In Geneva Dunant was able to convince four leading figures of the sense of his proposal. Together the five colleagues set about drawing up details for the proposed scheme, which they intended presenting for debate at an International Conference on Charity and Social Welfare to be held in Berlin.

At the last minute, Dunant independently added a significant extra proposal to the scheme, which he then circulated in the name of the 'Committee of Five', as they were by then known. His proposal, concerning the issue of neutrality, suggested that there should be international recognition of neutrality for military medical personnel and those who assisted them. His concept was simple: a wounded combatant should no longer be regarded as a soldier, but recognised instead as a wounded human being. It followed that anyone caring for these wounded men would require protection from the enemy while rendering assistance.

Shortly before the Berlin meeting was due to take place, the Conference was cancelled. It was then that the Committee of Five took what turned out to be a most momentous decision: they decided to host a conference themselves in Geneva. The purpose was to provide an international forum for debate on the proposals set out by the Committee. Invitations were extended to all European governments and the Conference took place in 1863. Agreement was reached on the article of neutrality and the Swiss flag in reverse was adopted as the symbol of protection. The Red Cross was born.

In the following year a more formal diplomatic conference was held at which 12 governments signed the first Geneva Convention for the Amelioration of the Condition of the Wounded and Sick in Armed Forces in the Field.

THE RED CROSS
IN BRITAIN

Pauline Samuelson

It was at the Geneva Conference of 1863 that a Resolution was passed on Henry Dunant's original idea described in his book *A Memory of Solferino* for national relief societies. The Resolution stated: 'There shall be in every country a Committee whose duty it will be to co-operate in time of war by all means in its power with the sanitary service of the army. This Committee shall organise itself in a manner which may appear to it as the most useful and expedient.'

As might be expected, the nations who had suffered most in wars were the first to respond to the Resolution. In 1866 the President of the International Committee of the Red Cross (ICRC), successor to the Committee of Five, wrote: 'England, Holland and Russia are now almost the only nations of the Old World where work has not yet been organised; but even in these, it numbers numerous adherents, and we may be sure that they will rally to it at no very distant period.'

There were indeed a number of adherents who were vocal in their support for a national relief committee in Britain. The cause had no stronger advocate than the Professor of Military Surgery at the Army Medical School, Netley – Professor Longmore – who had attended the diplomatic Geneva Conference. He made his views very clear in a lecture on the subject in 1866 when he said: 'No government in the world could afford to maintain a medical staff or provide the necessary means of meeting wants of such a battle as Solferino. . . . To supply these deficiencies was the part of the "National Committee" recommended by the Geneva Conference. Should this country remain without the formation of such a committee, it will find itself at a disadvantage as compared with neighbouring countries in case of becoming engaged in a great war.'

Others joined in the chorus to promote a National Committee. An article in the *Standard* newspaper cried, 'What is England doing? We have a Nightingale Fund for training nurses, our Patriotic Fund for the relief of Crimean sufferers. Where is our branch of the International Society for the Relief of the Sick and the Wounded? . . . Surely this is a slur on our national humanity, a blot on our fair escutcheon.'

In the event, a provisional committee was formed in 1868, mainly due to the persistence and energy of one man, John (later Sir John) Furley. The British Red Cross owes a particular debt of gratitude to this remarkable individual, for it is he more than any other person who should be credited with the introduction of the Red Cross to Britain.

The opportunity for the infant provisional committee to take its next step came hard on the heels of its foundation, and as a result of the outbreak of war in 1870 between the French and the Germans. Furley, still taking the initiative, approached a veteran of the Crimean campaign – the distinguished soldier Colonel Loyd-Lindsay, VC, who was a known champion of the Volunteer Movement. From that moment Colonel Loyd-Lindsay (later Lord Wantage) became the inspiration and natural leader of the Red Cross movement in this country. After his meeting with Furley in July 1870, he immediately wrote to *The Times* to announce that he had already placed £1,000 in the hands of his bankers to the credit of The Society for Aiding in Ameliorating the Condition of the Sick and Wounded in Time of War. 'If the money is not wanted,' he wrote, 'we shall all rejoice, but I fear that much more will be needed.'

Colonel Loyd-Lindsay proceeded to campaign among all the people he hoped would support the fledgling Society. Florence Nightingale, who earlier had been sceptical of Dunant's idea, responded through her brother-in-law, declaring the proposed Society to be 'quite on the right track'.

The Grand Prior of the Order of St John (which numbered among its members both John Furley and Professor Longmore), agreed to chair the meeting at which the National Society for Aid to the Sick and Wounded in War was formally launched. It owed its cumbersome title to the original wording drafted at the Conference in Geneva. It was more commonly known as the National Aid Society or simply as the Croix Rouge Anglaise or Red Cross Society.

During the first days of the Society's existence, the officers of the committee were chosen, the organisation was established and official government recognition was sought and given. Local fund-raising committees sprang up in nearly every large town in the United Kingdom, and gifts and donations flooded into the new offices in Trafalgar Square. The spectacular speed with which donated goods reached their ultimate destinations in the two war-torn countries was remarkable. During the Franco-Prussian War, for example, a makeshift French hospital's telegram request for 250 iron bedsteads was fulfilled within 48 hours. The beds arrived with a doctor who had spontaneously volunteered to accompany the consignment.

A month after the outbreak of the war, John Furley made one of his many trips to France where he travelled extensively through the battle-lines to see what relief needs and recruits should be mobilised by the National Society. Sixty-two British surgeons were sent to assist each side, and nurses also worked in both countries. Indeed, the value of volunteer nurses was praised by one eminent surgeon, who reported to the Society in London: 'I would not exchange one woman for a dozen men. . . . From the moment that women were involved as nurses, the whole aspect of our establishment was changed.'

Three months into the war, the Chairman of the Society, Colonel Loyd-Lindsay, was asked to deliver cheques representing donations of £20,000 each to the two warring parties. He also took 12 ambulance wagons with him, which had been funded by the military depot at Woolwich. His first stop was Le Havre, where he met another member of the Society, Lord Bury, who was buying horses and hiring drivers for the ambulances. On reaching Versailles, Loyd-Lindsay presented a cheque to the Prussian Chief Commissioner for Voluntary Aid. In the evening he dined with the King of Prussia. The next day he was given permission to enter the besieged city of Paris, where he was to hand over the other cheque to the Governor of Paris and the French War Minister.

Loyd-Lindsay's journey was fraught with risk, for no one knew how the red cross emblem of protection would be received. Although his progress was slow and spasmodic, culminating in a crossing of the Seine by small rowing boat, all went according to plan and he was eventually able to give the National Society in London a most impressive account of his experiences:

'The fact that I was conducted through lines of advanced posts by a Prussian Officer on my way to bring help to French sick and wounded could only have occurred under the protection of, and in the spirit of, the Geneva Convention. That I could make a journey from Havre to Paris in the course of which I had to pass through the advanced posts of both armies is, for men like me whose experience of war ante-dates the new order created by the Geneva Convention, a truly amazing thing. Nor did I have to wait as much as two minutes, and the white flag with the red cross was honoured by soldiers and patients alike. . . . The leaders of both sides acknowledge that the organisation for the sick and wounded in this war, which has already taken at least 100,000 lives on each side, has performed inestimable service.'

Today, 125 years after the British National Aid Society first fulfilled its humanitarian role, the British Red Cross Society remains an active and valued organisation throughout the United Kingdom.

To all who work for the Red Cross and Red Crescent Movement (see Appendix 1), the story of Solferino represents not so much a victory of one army over another, as a victory for the cause of humanity. Upon that battlefield was born the mission which today is carried out by millions of dedicated volunteers across the globe. Working in over 160 National Red Cross and Red Crescent Societies, Dunant's vision of a universal movement to give impartial help in time of war now extends far beyond the boundaries of the battlefield and stands as the world's largest humanitarian organisation.

The stories in this book recall the services offered by volunteers to just one of those many National Societies – the British Red Cross Society.

TROUBLE IN THE

BALKANS

Joyce Cary

Graduating from Oxford University in 1912, Joyce Cary, who was later to become a well-known novelist, went in search of adventure. Whereas the youth of today might volunteer for work with an aid agency, Cary chose to go to Montenegro where he could witness war at first hand. He later wrote about his experiences in Memoir of the Bobotes *(1964), from which the following is an extract.*

'I HAD A CERTAIN ROMANTIC ENTHUSIASM for the cause of the Montenegrins [fighting the Turkish forces in Europe]. For this campaign I had a little medal from the Montenegrin government, which I prize very much, though it was earned in what was, for a boy of my age, a holiday.'

Cary's work with the Red Cross came about largely by accident. He was arrested as a spy in Albania following an explosion in the arsenal where he found himself waiting. 'They let me go when I offered to help the Red Cross.' So it was that Cary joined a British Red Cross unit as a cook attached to the Montenegrin Army. The unit consisted of a medical student to look after the first aid field work, a number of volunteer orderlies, dressers and an interpreter. The British team kept near the battlefield, partly to give maximum help to the wounded and partly to be close to the solitary Swiss Red Cross doctor who was attached to a Montenegrin unit.

Daily living in the mountains of Montenegro was a far cry from the life of a privileged Oxford undergraduate before World War I. Joyce Cary described it thus: 'Anyone will tell you that war is not made up of fighting but of stew, and, if you are lucky, eggs. The affairs of the household are what count in war, even if the household only consists of no more than a billycan, a bundle of sticks to make a fire and a blanket.'

Of his everyday life in camp, cooking and helping with a constant succession of patients suffering from dysentery, fevers, coughs and sore feet, he wrote: 'They also came for the treatment of old wounds, frostbite and . . . nervous fancies. We slept in places nicely calculated between . . . other beds . . . piled high boxes of bandages . . . and the range of the interpreter's spit!'

Skirmishes broke out daily and the British team occupied itself with bringing in the wounded. Cary described the maxim guns at Dramos becoming very noisy: 'We guided ourselves by this noise and climbed straight across hedge, stream, thicket, bog and rock till we reached Dramos. There were many bullets flying down the road as we came along, and we found four wounded just brought in as we arrived. . . . I lit a fire and boiled the water; Lauder [the orderly], who could barely stand for fatigue, cleared the room of soldiers, spread sheepskins for his patients and made his examination. Two were hit in the legs, one thigh, one calf, no harm done, one in the forearm, the fourth was shot through the belly. The best thing that can happen for a man hit in the belly is to be forgotten. Let him alone, don't shake him and his gut will close up quickly. This man had been carried from Dramos, up and down three miles of stony hillsides and was lucky if he escaped peritonitis. We kept him three days on milk and he was better. Then his friends stole him and we never saw him again.'

Cary wrote a graphic description of his part in helping the wounded during the final assaults prior to the collapse of the Turkish Army: 'The first Turkish shrapnel burst over us when it was almost dark and the fire continued throughout the following day. By dawn we saw the first of the wounded straggling down the hill through open lines of the supports. We made a meal, waited for a burst of firing from the gunners to knock down the sharpshooters and went out towards the battleline. . . . I noticed the spring leaves falling off the trees and it took a moment's reflection to perceive that the bullets were cutting them down. We might have run – but it was not etiquette to run and very little good. . . .

'There were already many wounded crouched here and there. Lauder and I stopped to dress an old man – his right arm was shot to pieces. I suppose he was 70 years old, bent in the shanks, shaky about the chin, long white frieze coat (a clean one for the occasion) dabbled with blood, but he was perfectly collected and boasted that he had put his bomb in position and lighted it before he was hit. . . . We went on to the cottage and found the Captain driving a crowd of wounded under cover. I carried up the stores and sorted them, then went out for sticks for the fire. I stooped and pushed to and fro in the bushes. I came upon several wounded and sent them into the house. They were unaccustomed to find doctors about in battle and had been choosing quiet places to lie, according to their habit, until either they died or the fighting stopped and their friends came to take them away. . . .

'At midday there was a lull in the firing. I waited for a shell to burst and then went to the spring to wash. We were all in blood to the shoulders. . . . Finally we left in the dark. There was a little column of us that marched out. Two or three stretchers led the way, each on the shoulders of four men, others beside them carrying the bearer's rifle. Then came the medics with a sack of dressings; I came last with a stick on my shoulders and the lanterns tied to the end of the stick.'

WORLD WAR I

THE GREAT WAR

On 4 August 1914 news came like a thunderclap out of a clear summer sky that war was declared with Germany.

The country prepared itself for the struggle ahead; young men queued at recruitment offices in their eagerness to join the Army, and women offered their services to the nation. Auxiliary hospitals were quickly established by the Red Cross in vacant premises and other suitable buildings provided with the help of local authorities. The hospitals were under the control of the War Office and were frequently known as VAD hospitals.

The term 'VAD', which was the affectionate name given to wartime Red Cross and St John nurses, stood in fact for the units to which they belonged: Voluntary Aid Detachments. These Detachments came about in 1909 because a Territorial Army was formed to supplement the Regular Army in time of war. Its Medical and Nursing Reserves lacked sufficient personnel to cope with their new demands, so the British Red Cross, and later the Order of St John, were asked to raise Voluntary Aid Detachments to meet the expanding needs. The VAD Scheme was organised on a county basis, each county endeavouring to train as many men and women as possible.

By the outbreak of war in 1914 about 48,000 VADs were already serving in 1,800 Detachments. They gave help to the Army Medical Services by driving motor ambulances, nursing on ambulance trains and hospital ships, assisting at dressing and clearing stations and running auxiliary hospitals and convalescent homes. Some travelled to the front as 'Mobile VADs', while others remained at home to take over posts left vacant by those more qualified to meet urgent needs elsewhere.

By the Armistice of 1918, 90,000 Red Cross and 35,000 St John VADs had given service in some capacity. VADs had lost their lives in the bombing of the hospital at Étaples and in air raids at home. In all, 245 VADs were killed while on duty. It was probably the first time in the history of war that one could find a grave marked 'killed in action' and discover that the grave belonged not to a man but to a woman.

JOINING FORCES

Countess Mountbatten of Burma,

CBE, CD, JP, DL

Lady Mountbatten is a Vice President of the British Red Cross Society, having previously held many elected and distinguished offices since joining the Red Cross in 1948. In addition, she was Chairman of the Joint Committee of the Order of St John of Jerusalem and the British Red Cross Society for 10 years.

THE RELATIONSHIP BETWEEN THE British Red Cross Society and the Order of St John of Jerusalem is somewhat complicated. In order to explain it more clearly, I should like to sketch in some historical background which I hope will help people to understand the present-day existence of a Joint Committee of the Order and the Society.

In 1831, after a lapse of nearly three centuries, the Protestant Order of St John was revived in the British Realm. Its object was to provide help for the poor and needy. Consequently, when Henry Dunant's proposals for national relief societies were beginning to circulate around Europe, it is not surprising that among the first people to respond were members of the reconstituted Order of St John of Jerusalem.

Distinguished individuals like Professor Thomas Longmore and Sir John Furley were both members of the Order of St John. Together with Colonel Loyd-Lindsay as Chairman, a committee was formed with the intention of establishing a national Red Cross Society such as those already operating in other European countries.

With the outbreak of the Franco-Prussian War in 1870, the National Society for Aid to the Sick and Wounded in War went into action helping victims of both sides. This was the first time that the British Society used the new emblem of protection and neutrality – the red cross.

At the outbreak of the Boer War in 1899, the Red Cross Movement in Great Britain was still finding its feet. Therefore again, it was natural that the Central Committee of the Red Cross (which was formed to take responsibility for coordinating British voluntary aid to South Africa) should consist of a number of organisations, all of whom represented the humanitarian help available in the country at the time. The Army Nursing Reserve was part of the Central Committee, as was the St John Ambulance Association. Later in the war the St Andrew's Ambulance Association was represented, and the National Society for Aid to the Sick and Wounded in War, with experience of the Franco-Prussian conflict, also had representation in its own right. Each organisation had a specific contribution to make in the care of the sick and wounded, but all served under the banner of the Red Cross.

The early relationship between the Order and the Society established a pattern that was to be followed in all successive times of major international armed conflict. The coordinating committees of the Red Cross and St John (in peacetime the Order's name takes precedence, in wartime this is reversed) underwent several name changes over the course of various wars. For example, the Central British Red Cross Committee of the Boer War became the Joint War Committee during World War I, and the War Organisation during World War II. The principle of working together, however, remains the same. In 1951 an agreement defined a new structure for future cooperation between the Red Cross and St John in the event of war. Planning is currently coordinated through the National Voluntary Aid Societies' Emergency Committee.

The British Red Cross Society, the Order of St John of Jerusalem and the St Andrew's Ambulance Association are the officially recognised Voluntary Aid Societies as conceived by Henry Dunant so long ago. They are the instruments for carrying aid to the sick and wounded, supplementing the care given by medical services of the armed forces.

Through the years, both the Society and the Order have developed along their own lines. Each organisation retains its autonomy and its own special mission except in regard to the sick and wounded during times of conflict. Then, the two organisations work together under the red cross emblem and as part of the British Red Cross Society.

The distinctive characteristics of the two organisations are mainly due to the constitutional statutes upon which they were founded. The British Red Cross Society is a member of the International Red Cross and Red Crescent

Movement. It must comply with the principles as laid down by the International Conference of the Red Cross and Red Crescent, which has been the Movement's supreme governing body since the 19th century. It is both neutral and secular. The Order of St John of Jerusalem is a Christian order of chivalry, whose history and traditions would make it difficult to comply with some of the international requirements demanded of the Red Cross and Red Crescent Societies. This is a key reason for the two organisations remaining two separate charities, albeit working closely in many areas of common interest. The independence of each lends them greater strength and effectiveness. They have their own particular appeal and their close cooperation ensures that there is no wasted effort.

The origin of the present Joint Committee of the Order and the Society dates from its registration as a war charity in 1916. In order to continue joint peacetime schemes such as the Home Ambulance Service and other VAD activities needed for some years into the peace, an Act of Parliament was promulgated in 1918. In effect this gives the present Joint Committee authority to administer the residual assets held in its trust from the two world wars and to continue its primary work in support of service and ex-service personnel.

The Joint Committee is mainly concerned with awarding grants for the benefit of disabled and other ex-servicemen and women. During my time as Chairman, the categories eligible for grants were extended to include the families of ex-servicemen and women in need of help.

Since 1977 the Joint Committee has been responsible for the administration of Service Hospitals' Welfare Officers, who are either members of the Red Cross or St John, and whose role it is to care for the welfare needs of all service personnel in service hospitals in the United Kingdom and overseas. This service was initiated by the Red Cross during World War II and is now funded by the Ministry of Defence, with whom the Joint Committee works closely. The autonomy of the Joint Committee, however, remains intact, characterised by the lengthy and successful relationship between the Voluntary Aid Societies and the War Office, predecessor to the present Ministry of Defence.

Several generations on from the Red Cross Peace Library, set up at the end of World War I, the Joint Committee continues to administer the Hospital Library Service, which is a provision covering both service and civilian hospitals throughout England and Wales. Funding for the running of this service comes from a capitation arrangement with the Department of Health. The books are delivered by volunteers in nearly every county of England and Wales.

These activities, of common interest to both the Society and the Order, together with the ongoing statutory requirements demanded of both organisations as Voluntary Aid Societies, ensure a continuing close cooperation between the two charities. In time of peace they share mutual activities in the training field and in times of conflict both deliver their support for the benefit of the men and women who form the nation's armed services.

THE RED CROSS AND THE TIMES

Mary Ann Sieghart
Assistant Editor of The Times

THAT THE TIMES SHOULD BE CONTRIBUTING to this life and times of the British Red Cross is particularly appropriate. After all, it was this newspaper that acted as midwife to the birth of the organisation in 1870. At the outbreak of the Franco-Prussian War, a letter to the editor from Colonel Loyd-Lindsay, VC, led to the creation of a Red Cross Society in Britain: '. . . at the risk of being thought premature in my action,' wrote the Colonel, 'I have opened an account with Messrs Coutts to the credit of the Society for Aiding in Ameliorating the Conditions of the Sick and Wounded in Time of War.'

As a result of the letter being published in *The Times*, the British Red Cross was born. Almost immediately afterwards, *The Times* had reason to be grateful to the Society when one of its war correspondents, Colonel Kit Pemberton, was rescued by the Red Cross after being accidentally shot during the Battle of Bazeille in France.

The relationship was strengthened further when, following the onset of World War I, Lord Northcliffe speedily offered the support of *The Times* for fund-raising purposes. The newspaper proceeded to administer the entire Red Cross Appeal free of charge, acknowledging all donations and handling all publicity for the duration of the war. In total, *The Times* raised nearly £22,000,000 between 1914 and 1918.

The newspaper's attitude towards the Society generally, however, has not always been one of wholehearted approval. It was particularly critical when the South African Government delegation (not its Red Cross delegation) was suspended from the International Conference of the Red Cross held in 1986.

'This has been a bad weekend for one of the world's more respected and less controversial organisations,' said a leading article. 'For more than 100 years the International Red Cross has operated in war and peace, behind the battle lines of opposing armies, splendidly free of prejudice and the temptations of political partisanship. Its mission in South Africa, whose members are now awaiting instructions from Geneva following President Botha's notice to quit, have been involved in valuable work beyond the bounds of South Africa itself, securing the release of hostages taken by Unita in Angola, protecting the rights of political prisoners and caring for many thousands of refugees from the fighting in Mozambique. The intrusion of politics at its four-yearly conference in Geneva has not only spoilt a distinguished record but has awakened new fears for the future independence of the organisation.'

Those fears have not, fortunately, been realised. Since then, *The Times* has praised the Red Cross for its bravery in remaining in war zones when other Western organisations have left. And the International Committee of the Red Cross remains the institution that *Times* leader-writers most readily recommend for monitoring conditions in detention camps or for ensuring that aid reaches suffering civilians anywhere in the world. As long as it stays out of political controversy and continues to do sterling work, the Red Cross is likely to sustain our support in years to come.

Aboard an Ambulance Train, 1915–18

Percy O. Douglas (No. 4859)

Rejected as unfit for army service in the spring of 1915, I attached myself to the 25th County of London VAD (Camberwell Branch). I had heard rumoured that occasional calls were made for volunteers from Voluntary Aid Detachments to do service abroad and I was anxious to get overseas, like most young fellows at the time.

The Detachment met two or three times a week for lectures, practical instruction and drill. Each night also half a dozen men were picked in rotation for air-raid duties. Sometimes on meeting nights I missed familiar faces and was told that they had gone to France. As the weeks went by I began to wonder when my turn was coming.

It came on Friday 23 July 1915. I was summoned by a telephone message to call at the British Red Cross Society's headquarters in Pall Mall. So to Pall Mall I went. First I saw a Lady Commandant, in charge of my papers, who asked me if I was willing to go overseas. Then I went to the Orderlies' Office, where a doctor examined me. He explained that the Red Cross did not want to encourage men that were fit to be trained for the army proper, and that he had to satisfy himself that people who volunteered for the BRCS were not trying to escape service in the Army. The doctor eventually put his signature to my papers, which enabled me to collect chits for my kit the following day.

On 9 August I received my 'marching orders' to sail on Friday the 13th. To the more superstitious both the day of the week and the day of the month would have been ill omens. For me, though, the day was brimful of excitement. It was also a time of sadness at parting with those who were very dear.

We were as mixed a crew as could be got together. Miners from Durham and Wales, factory hands from Manchester, clerks from London and Nottingham and a Wesleyan parson. We mustered about 50, including a major in the Royal Army Medical Corps who was the Officer Commanding, two BRCS doctors, a matron and two nursing sisters. We arrived at Boulogne after a rather uncomfortable journey on the wooden slatted seats of a French third-class carriage and were greeted cordially by the personnel already in Boulogne.

The train accommodation was composed of one officers' ward and three stretcher-case wards for NCOs and men, each with room for 30 patients. At opposite ends of the train there were 30 carriages for the use of 240 sitting or less serious cases. Amidships were officers' and sisters' quarters, the NCOs' mess and the orderlies' mess, two cookhouses, a storeroom, the OC's office, a dispensary, an operating theatre and the orderlies' sleeping quarters. We were certainly well equipped.

The next day we steamed out of Abbeville on our first journey to collect the wounded.

There are too many memories for me to write them all. I remember an early journey when we were collecting the powerful fellows from the 1st Gordon & King's Own Scottish Border Regiments. Lifting some of these chaps on to the topmost beds in the train with the minimum of discomfort to them tested my strength to the hilt.

Then there was the time when we kicked our heels and uttered expletives when a defective wheel on the train held us up for a whole week. We spent the time polishing and repolishing all that was polishable while we waited to be on our travels again.

Occasionally, the journeys were quite short, but more often than not they lasted many hours. The Tommies were generally very happy to get on an ambulance train for the simple reason that it was a stage nearer home for them. We got used to the inevitable first question: 'Where are we going, chum?' So we would find out our destination before we started on a journey. If we were bound for Le Havre or Boulogne, chances were the wounded would catch an early boat to Blighty; if we were headed for Rouen or Étaple, then it was a base hospital.

Calls were made on us at all times of the day and night, so it was essential to make the wards ready for receiving another load of patients immediately a batch had been unloaded. The 'making ready' entailed making beds, sweeping and washing the floors, cleaning the food and surgical receptacles, taking on water and re-provisioning fatigues.

From August to December before my first leave we carried 8,000 patients on our Train No. 17. Although we often felt quite worn out after the long days and nights, we found joy in our tiredness at having been able to render a service to those who were suffering and needed our help.

VERA BRITTAIN — A RED CROSS MEMOIR

The Rt. Hon. Baroness Williams of Crosby P. C.

'You see,' my mother said, 'that's how you make a hospital corner.' In our house all the sheet corners were neatly folded into triangles and then tucked under the mattress, leaving never a ruckle or bump in the linen. My mother's lesson in hospital corners had been learned in a hard school, the school of being a Red Cross VAD in World War I.

Hospital corners weren't the only legacy of that experience. My mother, Vera Brittain, author of a famous book on the war called *Testament of Youth*, learned punctuality, precision and patience too. She also learned deeper things about human suffering and human courage, and about how to live through the worst times by hard work and taking one day at a time.

Nursing for her was in part a way of numbing herself to pain, particularly the pain of repeated bereavements. Only by plunging into helping others stricken by injury or mutilation could she find a purpose in living. 'I thought of nothing at all except the thing I was going to do next,' she wrote in *Chronicle of Youth*, her World War I diary.

Nurses were idealised by the soldiers and by the public. My mother describes her journey home in 1917, travelling from Malta, where she served in an army hospital, across France, with the troops waving and cheering as the nurses travelled by.

But life on the wards was a long way away from the idealised picture. Matrons were not questioned, equipment was primitive and VADs were the lowest in a long and rigid hierarchy. 'Dust the wards, wash the doctor's tables and get hot water in the jugs!' was one among many orders my mother recalled, for much VAD nursing was basically hard domestic work.

My mother learned that personality and temperament were as important to nurses as professional skills. 'Adaptability, sympathy and magnetism of temperament,' she wrote in her diary, 'count for more than the ability to bandage or to make foods.'

Nurses in those days were very much the handmaidens of doctors, and doctors were gods. Today nursing is recognised as a vital complement to the work of doctors, and we increasingly realise the contribution nurses make to general practices as well as to hospital care. As medicine becomes more holistic in its approach, we come to appreciate that the nurse's relationship with patients can be an important element in their recovery. Too much emphasis on performance and speed of handling cases could undervalue this crucial human element in the nurse–patient relationship.

The Red Cross, like nursing generally, has moved on since my mother's day. As well as extending its services in this country, the Movement has emphasised its international nature through its commitment to helping the victims of violence, war and natural disasters wherever they may be. It has somehow retained its professional detachment from partisan and national positions.

Though medical expertise has moved on, the need for the Red Cross is as great as ever. In our post Cold War world we seem to have inherited scores of unresolved conflicts – national, ethnic, religious, communitarian. The human race still has far to go to learn how to resolve disputes peacefully.

In the long and bitter years of our learning, the Red Cross continues to be an example to politicians, governments and military commanders of how it can be done. I saw a little of its work last year in Bosnia and Croatia, countries where the courage and dedication of aid workers and the kindliness of many ordinary civilians go some way to offset the awful record of brutality and savagery among the armies and the guerrilla bands.

My mother dedicated herself to the pursuit of peace because of what she saw and learned as a wartime Red Cross nurse. The Red Cross itself continues to heal the wounds of war and violence, and to work for a better world.

THE RED CROSS BLOKE

The following poem was written in Mildred Perry's autograph book during World War I. It is reproduced here by kind permission of her daughter, Mrs C.M. Hurley of Langport, Somerset.

The Red Cross 'Bloke.

Not a blinkin' rap do we care for the chaps
With the Red Cross sign on his sleeve.
Till we get to the Front an the "stand to" stunt
An' a farewell bomb when we leave.
'Midst that flyin' death, you hold your breath,
An' life seems suddenly dear.
While the Red Cross Chap, is out of the scrap
In the safest Part — at the rear.

My own turn came — its part of the game,
In a Scrap we had before Loos.
When the blinkin' Huns tried to pinch the guns
Of the 15th — never mind whose
They's tried, an' tried, an' you bet they'd died
While we lost many a Chum.
Till word came through, "now lads, stand to!"
An' the next was, "Here they come!"
We charged and yelled an' the line was held
But I cant remember the rest
For the earth spun round an' I hit the ground
With daylight inside my chest

When next I awoke, a 'Red Cross Bloke
    Was crossing that zone of death.
An' I watched him come through that shrapnel hum
    Just watched an' held my breath.
Till he reached my side, with a crawl an' glide
    An' I blest his crimson Crest,
"For he made me snug with a comfy plug
    On the painful hole in my chest
Then away he crept an' I must have slept
    "For when I awoke with the pain,
I was back at the Base as a Hospital case
    An' was booked through to "Blighty" again

—— :,: ——

We landed alright on a wet, stormy night
    But what did I care for the rain
When a Red Cross Bloke fixed me up with a smoke
    An' a crib on a Red Cross Train ?.
An' thats how I'm here feelin' shaky an' queer
    In this clinkin' Red Cross bed
With a Red Cross hearse, when I'm feelin worse
    To lay cool things on my head.
An' all of it seems to be part of my dreams
    But I know that its not been a hoax
"For there's thousands today who are ready to say
    "Thank God for the 'Red Cross Blokes."

—— :,: ——

From "Spat's Tunes"
    Saturday Aug: 14th 1916

Dorothy A Barker
Sept: 1916

29

THE FRONT LINE, 1916

The following extract comes from an unknown regimental journal and was originally published in the Red Cross Journal of 1917.

'MOST PEOPLE HAVE A POPULAR NOTION that the Red Cross gives merely provision in hospitals and that it is hardly concerned with the wounded man until he reaches hospital.

'The wounded man arrives at the battalion aid post where he is first attended to with hot tea – probably from a Red Cross urn. Even the electric torch which has helped with his first aid dressing is probably a Red Cross gift.

'At the advanced dressing station he certainly received a Red Cross cigarette, and, if lightly wounded, a Red Cross walking stick to replace his rifle. The motor ambulance, which conveyed him to the main dressing station, bore the Red Cross legend and was probably a gift from some county branch. Oil stoves, lamps and the dressing pyjamas to make him comfortable all have the marks of the Red Cross upon them.'

RETREAT FROM CAPORETTO, 1917

Freya Stark

Freya Stark, the distinguished travel writer who died in 1993 aged 100, served as a VAD nurse on the Italian front with the Trevelyan Ambulance Unit. This was a hospital housed in George Trevelyan's Villa Trento near Undine.

'THE VILLA TRENTO WAS A HAPPY PLACE and everyone adored George Trevelyan for his chivalry and devotion. . . . The routine of the unit largely depended on what was happening at the front. . . . When an offensive was on, our drivers took no rest day or night, ambulances arrived at every hour. We evacuated as soon as we could to the base hospital in Undine; otherwise we kept our people, mostly wounded with shell splinters, and watched their wounds closing day by day round the little rubber drain pipes.'

Being the only British unit in the area, the Trevelyan Unit was given the honour of being the last hospital left to function before the catastrophic retreat from Caporetto when the Italians were routed by the Austrians. Freya Stark's diary records those last days.

26th Oct. 1917

This has been a very long, eventful day. In the morning an order came to clear the hospital of all patients. We had a great rush to get our fractures dressed and into their uniforms while ambulance after ambulance drove up to carry them all away. The guns were pounding at slow intervals nearer than yesterday it seemed. We stripped and dismounted the beds that were to go to the rear with some of our VADs. Our stretcher cases have not yet all cleared off. Poor little Celeste with his amputated leg and arm sat and shivered with nervousness!

The rumours meanwhile were most various. Rava, it seems, is really lost. Caporetto also went and the Austrians reached the River Isona at Canale. The road in front here was a sad sight all day – one long, dejected stream of soldiers, guns, endless Red Cross ambulances, women and children, carts with household goods, and always more guns and more soldiers – all going toward the rear.

Our ward now has three bad cases in beds, and 20 on the mattresses along the floor; nobody is allowed to undress as we may have to leave suddenly. The news tonight is still bad. Gorizia expected to fall tomorrow. Our cars have been carrying refugees today – streams of them all leaving Undine in panic as fast as they can.

Am now going to sleep with the chance of being called any time in the night to leave and the Austrians about nine miles away.

27th Oct., afternoon

Were not roused in the night after all and Bosy's precaution of sleeping with her hair done up turned out unnecessary; after all, one may as well be captured in one's nightgown as in one's corsets, so I undressed completely and got what sleep was possible with the horrible stream of retreating men tramping below the windows.

Today we live in uncertainty of our future. But we are the last hospital to move which is satisfactory. Meanwhile, we remain here to collect what wounded there are, although most have been taken prisoners. We only get a few stragglers, and now those cases have cleared off as well. We have nothing to do. The weather is lovely – a golden autumn day.

28th Oct. in Car No. 88

Yesterday Matron told us to be ready at once to start for Conegliano to prepare the new hospital there. . . . We had tea, and the whistle called us to start on the retreat.

We left at 5:15, a wonderful evening. The hospital quite empty. Through the twilight till the moon came up, a few shells sounding behind us. The road packed with traffic three deep, carabinieri all along to keep order; all talking, shouting, or very tired. One got more and more to feel it as a retreat. We got stuck for half hours at a time, the whole road lined with tired figures sleeping anywhere in heaps on banks . . .

We have now been travelling 20½ hours and are only 16 kilometres from

Undine. For one stretch the two columns were distinct, one for horses, the other for motors. But then comes a jumble and we just wait till the thing ahead moves a few yards. . . . We had sandwiches of potted sausage between two sweet biscuits and cold plum pudding at about 2 a.m. . . . all squashed into the ambulance with rain and wind buffeting outside. The men and refugees all come to look in at us and want to have a lift but we are already over-weighted. . . . The flares of the explosions are visible all along the sky.

The retreat continued, pausing briefly in Padua on 29 October. On 1 November Car No. 88 reached Milan.

Nov. 1st
We heard yesterday that the hospital was finished as all our equipment is lost. I offered myself at once to Dr Brock to work in an Italian place for the rush that is bound to come. The matter was laid before the Commando Supremo by Lord Monson, but an order came saying all English nurses were to be got away.

Today I said good-bye to all. Trevvy [George Trevelyan] said we VADs had done well in the retreat. I told him we would go to whichever end of the world he sent us, and so we would.

The Royal Star and Garter Home

Simon Weston

T HE NAME 'Star and GARTER' has been known on Richmond Hill in Surrey for over 200 years. First there was a pub by that name, which was a famous landmark for travellers arriving in London. Then, in 1865, a hotel was built to replace the pub. Many people, from Queen Victoria to Dickens, visited the hotel in its heyday, but by World War I it had stood empty for some years.

In 1915 Queen Mary, consort of King George V, became very concerned about the number of paralysed and permanently war-wounded men who had nowhere to go once they had been discharged from hospital. So, when the Auctioneers' and Estate Agents' Institute raised the funds to buy the crumbling hotel and offered it to Queen Mary, she gratefully accepted their gift. She then entrusted the British Red Cross Society to run it as a home for disabled soldiers and sailors.

At first it was hoped to adapt the old building, but eventually it had to be pulled down. A magnificent new home was opened by Queen Mary in 1925 'as a permanent haven for disabled ex-servicemen'. The new emblem of the home included the old star and the red cross in recognition of its governing body.

Everyone who has enjoyed the privilege of visiting this home will know why it has a special place in my heart. I was recovering from burns I received in the Falklands War when I first met some of the remarkable residents who live in the Royal Star and Garter Home. Each time I go back there I meet determined men and women of all ages who show no hint of bitterness for their disabilities. Like me, they were all in the services and like me many of them were simply doing their duty when their lives were dramatically turned upside-down in a split second of enemy action.

Today the Royal Star and Garter has its own Royal Charter and is home to

200 men and women, all of whom served in the forces or reserves. It is a large mixed community, with some residents needing permanent nursing care. Others stay for just a few months to use the exceptional rehabilitation facilities and to learn how to cope after, say, a stroke or other debilitating illness. Still others spend just a couple of weeks away from their own homes while their relatives take a holiday.

The magnificent building and the special dedication of everyone involved in caring for the residents make the Royal Star and Garter unique. It can truly be called a *home* in every sense of the word.

BETWEEN THE WARS

PEACETIME YEARS

Caroline Moorehead

Author and film-maker Caroline Moorehead is currently writing a history of the ICRC. Her previous subjects include the life of Bertrand Russell and human rights.

'BEYOND THE ROAR OF THE GUNS, the rumble of the ambulance wagons and the tramp of men, they have reached a country where all is still and, in the midst of war, have found that peace that passeth all understanding.' With these fulsome words, delivered in the summer of 1919, the British Red Cross Society honoured its war dead. Like other national Red Cross societies around the world, the British had had its share of missing and wounded, and now remembered them with stoicism, affection and not a little sentimentality. But there was a good deal of understandable pride too. The Red Cross Movement had gone into World War I untested in fighting on such a scale. It had emerged admired, highly professional and extremely proficient, its skills recognised in all 28 countries that had gone to war. The question the societies now faced was what came next. They had proved their worth in war: could they do the same in peace?

No Red Cross Society had been more active, especially in the last two years of war, than that of the United States. Surgeons, nurses, administrators, drivers and canteen workers had swept into Europe with the arriving American Army, bringing supplies, food and equipment. It was not surprising, then, that the impetus for post-war action came from an American, Henry Davison, President of the War Committee of the American Red Cross. Davison was a successful banker and a much-liked man, under whose leadership the American Red Cross had grown from 300,000 members in 1914 to 28 million in 1918. Long before the fighting stopped, Davison was saying that the

Red Cross Societies should set about helping governments relieve the distress and destitution caused by four years of war. He urged them to come to grips with peacetime 'pestilence, famine and death, and clean up the world and do away with illness and suffering'. More than that, they should forge closer links with one another, to coordinate rather than duplicate their activities, and to act as a moral force in the post-war world, calling for lasting peace and an end to war itself.

What Davison had in mind was an idea that had been talked about often in the early years of the century – some kind of federation of national societies, to complement but not replace the International Committee of the Red Cross, whose status as keeper of the Geneva Conventions and spiritual backbone of the Movement no one contested. Like the great pioneers before him, Davison was a man in a hurry, driven by a sense of urgency. To launch his 'international charity organisation' he held a dinner at the Palais d'Orsay Hotel in Paris on 21 February 1919, which was attended by government representatives, diplomats, luminaries of the arts and sciences, and journalists from a hundred newspapers. Within three months a League of Red Cross Societies had been officially constituted in Paris, ready to associate the existing national societies throughout the world and guide new ones in the right direction.

Relations with the long-standing and rather conservative ICRC were not always easy, however, and it was not until 1928, nine years later, that the ICRC's suspicions about the new organisation were finally allayed. This was achieved by drawing clear demarcation lines between the two bodies and establishing a joint liaison committee to ensure harmony.

As it turned out, the National Societies need not have wondered how they would fill their peacetime days. The Armistice had indeed brought a halt to fighting, but Europe was in ruins. Millions of former prisoners of war were stranded, many of them in Russia, where 2 million men were still stuck in camps, idle and desperate. Spanish influenza, typhus, cholera and tuberculosis developed among people too malnourished to fight disease. While Red Cross leaders settled down to meetings, resolutions, drafts and proposals, their members went on doing what they did best – taking food, supplies and medicine to those who needed them, regardless of race and political persuasion.

Natural disasters then claimed their attention. The 1920s and 1930s were marked by a series of earthquakes, floods and other catastrophes, but by now the machinery of mutual help between sister societies was well oiled. The earthquake that hit Tokyo and Yokohama in 1923 claimed 200,000 lives and made 2 million people homeless, but 35 separate societies were quick to rally. They rallied again, whenever and wherever misfortune fell.

At home, in their own countries, National Societies looked around and took stock. The war had brought to light the extreme unhealthiness of much of the world's population. Of the men called up in 1917 and 1918 in Britain, only one in three had been fit for active service. Poor diet, appalling working conditions and unsanitary housing were producing anaemia, rickets and tuberculosis. As a result of these findings, preventative medicine, in the shape of health education, took over from making bandages. By 1922 a vast junior Red Cross had been born, with members in 25 countries. The idea was to involve children in what the Japanese Red Cross called 'the spirit of self-sacrifice' and what children in the USA named a 'health crusade'.

While the war had tested Red Cross skills in medicine and nursing, peace was to provide a greater challenge: no less than the reform of society itself. Month after month the Bulletin of the League ran articles on tuberculosis, nutrition, blindness, venereal diseases, the 'danger of the rat', lice, dental hygiene, alcoholism, sunstroke and the traffic in opium. No issue was too big or too small. New concerns, such as town planning and 'first aid on highways', reflected the changing world, but politics were firmly ignored. Help was given to refugees, but the circumstances that led to their situation were not discussed. Nowhere is the mood of the League – resolute and idealistic in its 'titanic battle' against human distress and disease – more apparent than in its monthly bulletins, though it is not hard to spot intimations of the tragedy that would soon engulf Europe.

The last great gathering of Societies, before the world turned once again to war, was held in London in June 1938. The 16th International Conference was attended by 54 National Societies and, like previous international gatherings, was held with considerable panache. Evening dress and decorations were worn for receptions, and morning coat and tails for Buckingham Palace. Talk at the conference was of peace, goodwill and the fellowship of man, but no issue was more anxiously debated than that of protecting civilians in the event of war. If the conflicts of the 1920s and 1930s had proved anything, it was the vulnerability of ordinary people, what Norman Davis, Chairman of the League's Board of Governors, called the 'revolting and needless slaughter and maiming of helpless women and children'.

Draft resolutions about prohibiting the bombing of towns and the setting up of immunity zones were drawn up and circulated over several months, but it was too late. World events moved faster than the interminable deliberations of Red Cross officers. World War II broke out, leaving civilians as unprotected as they had always been. It was to take Nazi atrocities in occupied Europe to bring about international legislation governing non-combatants. But that was all much later. In the summer of 1938, as the conference delegates returned to their various countries thinking how well their societies had handled 20 years of peace, many must have been asking themselves how ready they were again for war.

Work Between the Wars

Claire Rayner

At the end of World War I the British Red Cross found itself facing a dilemma: what use was it going to make of its huge organisation in peacetime?

For some time after the Armistice there was still plenty to do in auxiliary hospitals and convalescent homes. But gradually, as the casualties mercifully ceased to arrive, these establishments were no longer needed in such numbers.

In London the Joint War Committee started to wind down, and one by one the important departments, which had been so vital during the war, closed. This left thousands of VAD volunteers at a loose end. What was to become of that wealth of goodwill and training?

By 1920 the whole Red Cross Movement was seriously developing its peacetime role. In Britain Queen Alexandra wrote to *The Times*, setting out her views on what she thought the British Red Cross ought to be doing. She wrote that obviously its first task was to continue looking after the thousands of sick and wounded ex-servicemen who needed help – what we today would call 'care in the community'. However, the Queen also recommended some new jobs for the Red Cross. She was keen that they should raise local funds in order to pioneer services in infant and child welfare, and give special help to crippled children. She also suggested they help start a local motor ambulance service that would help those far from hospitals, and pointed out the help they could give to those suffering from the scourge of that period – tuberculosis. In short, she set out a whole peacetime agenda for the Society.

Briefly, here are some examples of the services pioneered by the Red Cross during the inter-war years.

Home Service Ambulance

Can you imagine what it must have been like in the days before there was a national ambulance service? We may complain about our beloved NHS, but what must it have been like when no simple telephone call could summon help?

After World War I a scheme was devised whereby all wartime ambulances no longer needed at the front would be used in rural areas. Some 500 motor vehicles were distributed by the Joint War Committee to the Red Cross and St John Ambulance Brigade all over England and Wales. In Scotland the Red Cross handed over a large number of ambulances to St Andrew's Ambulance Association.

The service was run very much along Joint Committee lines, with the men of St John specialising in first aid and accident care and the Red Cross using their predominantly female VADs for non-emergency journeys.

The service was funded by several sources – local authorities, trade unions and voluntary public donations – and the Red Cross and St John volunteers gave their time rather as voluntary firemen do today. Ambulances were stationed at factories and mining sites in case of accidents, but also, if necessary, carried sick people to hospital.

The important point was that the volunteers were *trained*, which not only gave the patients confidence but also helped the doctors treating them. The 'sick wagon' gave way to the *hôpital ambulant* (from the French, meaning mobile hospital), and this later led to the modern word 'ambulance'.

Clinics for Adults and Children

As the post-war clinics that treated servicemen became less needed, they were converted for civilian use. These clinics were scattered all over the country and were known by various names in different Red Cross branches – Orthopaedic Clinics, Massage Clinics, Cripples' Care Clinics, Rheumatism Clinics.

Physicians and surgeons referred patients to these clinics if they did not need hospital treatment, or could not afford to go to hospital because of the loss of earnings which this incurred. With so little rural transport available, the local clinics were a godsend for small communities and hard-pressed families. Early physiotherapy techniques and electrical therapies, such as ultra-violet radiation and diathermy, were used in many of the treatments, and both children and adults were helped for complaints ranging from rheumatism and rickets to infantile paralysis and bow legs.

In most clinics specialists and GPs gave their services free. When this was not the case, fees for nurses and doctors were often paid by the County Education Committees. The School Medical Service depended heavily on the Red Cross to organise clinics and provide extra staff in the form of volunteers. These clinics provide an early example of cooperation between a voluntary organisation and the statutory authorities. They also show the pioneering role of the Red Cross and the care the Society takes to avoid funding provisions which are by law the obligation of the State. The Red Cross role has always been to give supplementary support.

Early Community Care

The main area of community care, which involved VADs across the country, was the beginning of the Infant and Child Welfare Movement. In 1923 a Central Council was formed, bringing together under the Red Cross all sections of care for child welfare. Infant Welfare Centres and Day Nurseries were started, and in some cases the local Red Cross Detachment took full responsibility for running the centres. In others, they handled anything from administration to transport needs, organised cooking and hygiene classes for mothers and supervised the weighing and care of the babies.

Another development to come from the years immediately following World War I was the scheme launched by the Ministry of Pensions for a nationwide network of cottage hospitals. In many cases these were called 'memorial hospitals' as they were raised by public subscription in memory of those who died in the war. Red Cross VADs were involved both practically and on the management committees in the new hospitals.

In 1921 a Division of the London Red Cross launched its first depot for loaning 'sickroom and invalid requisites' to those sick at home or needing equipment after discharge from hospital.

Funding Research

Years ago, when there were fewer registered charities, organisations like the Red Cross, which were well established and respected, were asked to raise funds on behalf of new causes. In 1923 the Provisional Executive Council of the British Empire Cancer Campaign invited the British Red Cross to launch and run an appeal for £1 million to fund cancer research throughout the Empire.

This was the first fundraising campaign ever to be launched for cancer research. Its target was £1 million and 2 per cent of the proceeds were to go to the British Red Cross for its own services. Its trustees included representatives from the Royal Society and the Medical Research Council.

Red, Cross Lady.

Redder, crosser Ladies.

Reddest, crossest Ladies.

THE EARLY BLOOD TRANSFUSION SERVICE

Professor Sir Magdi Yacoub and Dr Marcela Contreras

For those of us whose work necessitates close contact with the present-day National Blood Transfusion Service, or, indeed, for those who owe their lives to it, the origins of the Service are of special interest because they show what can happen as the result of a pioneering idea and the dedication of a single volunteer.

Seventy years ago Britain led the way in developing a voluntary blood donors' system which has had far-reaching effects across the world. Today's highly sophisticated National Blood Transfusion Service, with its processing, preservation and advanced testing facilities, research and development, as well as international links, has come a long way from the simple concept of an individual donor providing blood direct to the needy recipient. In essence, however, the system remains unchanged, for the Blood Transfusion Service still depends largely on the support of the people of this country.

This story begins in 1921 with a telephone call from King's College Hospital in London to the Camberwell Division of the Red Cross, desperately asking if someone could be found who would give a pint of blood to a seriously ill patient. Percy Lane Oliver, honorary secretary of the division, acted promptly and four Red Cross members sped to the hospital as fast as they could go. Alas, before the transfusion could take place, the patient died.

A few months later a similar request came from another hospital, and in this case the transfusion was carried out successfully.

News spread fast, and as further applications began to come in, Percy Oliver decided to form a permanent panel of donors in the London area who could quickly provide the required blood group at any time to any hospital or nursing home requesting it. By 1923 six hospitals were using donors, and 24 regular volunteers were available to go straight to the hospitals where blood was needed.

Demand soon outgrew the capability of Camberwell Division's existing donor membership, so it was decided to seek more donors by appealing in a local newspaper. A dozen offers resulted, one of which was from a local Rover Scout. This led to more Rover Scouts volunteering, and made Percy Oliver confident enough to launch the Greater London Red Cross Blood Transfusion Service.

The Red Cross in Camberwell continued to run the service, with 24-hour telephone access staffed by volunteers, until 1925. Then it became evident that the task was growing too large for the hard-pressed Camberwell Division, so the Greater London Red Cross Blood Transfusion Service was transferred to the National Headquarters of the Society.

In 1927 around 1,000 calls for blood were answered, with 68 hospitals using directly summoned donors when needed. Donors continued to come primarily from Rover Scouts and Red Cross members, although other organisations, such as Toc H (Talbot House) and the YMCA, also became active in recruiting donors. People were called in from as far afield as the south coast, Berkshire and Hertfordshire. St Bartholomew's Hospital in the City of London was the most frequent user of the Service, with 138 calls being registered in one year.

No charge was made by the Transfusion Service, but donations were gratefully received towards the running costs of Red Cross National Head-quarters' administration. Funds were set aside for reimbursing donors' lost earnings and travel expenses, but few claimed the money. As today, donors appreciated the refreshments provided after the session.

Most remarkable was the speed with which donors were able to reach the hospital: the average time from telephone request to arrival was only half an hour. Frequently this was even less when the donor was a volunteer working in the Blood Transfusion Office itself. The GPO recognised the importance of the Transfusion Service by issuing special instructions to telephone operators to clear the lines and arrange rapid connections for hospital requests.

By the end of the 1920s Percy Oliver was beginning to receive enquiries from other countries seeking information and advice on organising similar blood donation schemes. The USA, Germany, Australia and the West Indies were among the first to adopt their own blood donor services modelled on the London pattern.

In the early days the organisation had to proceed by trial and error, and no safe interval between donations had been established. Procedures and safe-guards for hospitals and other institutions using the Service were gradually formulated. The Service, however, did stipulate three things from the outset: venesection (the collection of blood from a vein) could only be undertaken by qualified doctors; the technique known as needle puncture was prohibited; and the blood group of the patient had to be specified so that only a donor of the same group was approached.

In 1934 further progress was made when the Transfusion Service appointed a part-time medical officer. He worked in the Pathology Department of a London teaching hospital, which enabled him to carry out medical examinations and standard grouping techniques on each newly recruited donor. Donors were re-examined after every 10 transfusions and valuable data was collected about the interval that should elapse between blood donations. The age limits of 18 to 65 were also established and many of the recommendations and procedures set out by the Greater London Red Cross Blood Transfusion Service remain the basis upon which blood transfusion services function to this day in many parts of the world.

The Munich Crisis in 1938 alerted people to the imminent possibility of war and led to some profound changes in the service. The first of these was a plan to establish a 'blood bank', which could store large quantities of blood. This was made possible by scientific advances, which had discovered how to preserve the essential properties of blood and store it for transfusion. Thus, except when very rare blood groups were needed, the old system of calling up donors to supply individual transfusions was no longer necessary.

The emergency system speedily devised to meet the 1938 crisis worked thus: an ambulance station situated in the suburbs of London was cleared as a donor centre and a team of local doctors was recruited to take the donations. Three ambulances were on hand to deliver blood wherever needed, and London hospitals were advised to make preparations for its storage. Medical men connected with the service agreed to form a rota to deal with the administrative work. Notices were prepared for the press and the BBC, appealing for donors to give blood and providing details of how to reach the centre. A well-known dairy offered to supply their obsolete milk bottles to hold the blood, and large refrigerators, holding 1,000 bottles each, were installed underground. This meant that large quantities of blood could be stored safely at the centre, ready for use in the anticipated emergency.

The enormous growth of blood transfusion during World War II made it imperative for the State to undertake permanent responsibility for providing blood products, standard apparatus for taking and giving blood throughout the country and for testing and grouping blood units. A National Blood Transfusion Service was eventually established in 1946, with regional centres in London and other major cities in England and Wales. Scotland had a head start, with five transfusion centres established there in 1940.

Today the Red Cross continues the tradition of providing donors for the National Blood Transfusion Service, but its members also contribute in other important ways. Many act as local organisers of donor sessions, or act as ancillary helpers at sessions in their county branches. They are also active in helping to recruit new donors.

Percy Oliver's inspiration and enthusiasm in 1921 has gone a long way towards establishing one of the best National Blood Transfusion Services in the world, fully dependent on unpaid, voluntary donors. There are 13 transfusion centres in England, five in Scotland, one in Wales and one in Northern Ireland, collecting a total of more than 2.5 million units of blood each year. The advent of preservative solutions and plastic collection packs have facilitated the processing of most of this blood into different components so that a single donation can benefit more than one patient: red cells for the treatment of anaemia, platelets for the treatment of bleeding disorders, and plasma components to replace missing clotting factors. Tonnes of plasma are fractionated at two plants in Elstree and Edinburgh for the production of clotting factors, albumin and immunoglobulins. Modern medicine and surgery are reliant on the vast number of blood derivatives currently available from the Blood Transfusion Service. It would, for example, be impossible to treat leukaemia or haemophilia, or to perform advanced cardiac surgery without the unconditional support of blood donors who are still following the example set by the Camberwell Division of the British Red Cross.

THE EARLIEST BRING &
BUY SALE

BRITISH RED CROSS SOCIETY
An American Tea
will be held at
The Borough Hall, Guildford
On Tuesday Feb. 7th, 1928

The Treasurer and the Commandant
Were sitting hand in hand;
They wept like anything to see
The bare and naked land;
'If we could only raise some funds,'
They said, 'it would be grand.

'For how on earth can we expect
To train our motley crew
Without equipment adequate,
And drills and lectures too?
All our recruits are keen enough
But pence are far too few.'

Then suddenly a crashing wave
Of inspiration came.
'I've got it,' said the Treasurer,
'I know a splendid game.
We'll have a tea (American)
Of world-renown-ed fame.

'We've only got to ask our friends
To bring a bob – or more.
One pays for tea, and all the rest
Will go to swell our store.
They buy – and bring – a parcel too,

One bob's worth or two score!'

'We'll have it,' said the Commandants
In accents firm and low.
'And after tea we'll offer them
A first-rate, All-Star Show;
And then they'll see we really are
More grateful than they know.'

A Red Cross Menu

The following menu, served at the Annual Dinner of Middlesex VAD/49 (Men), in 1930, was strongly flavoured with sports and first aid – abiding interests of the Red Cross to this day.

Soup – Red Cross.
Dissected Sole.
Wembley Sauce.
Fractured Potatoes.
Roast Beef of Middlesex and Yorkshire.
Lamb Fractured Femur.   49th Sauce.
Drilled Peas.
Potatoes.
Commandant's Tart.
Officer's Sauce.
Contused Trifle.
Stadium Cheese.   Greyhound Biscuits.
Café à la Cup Final.
Wines.   Minerals.
Stretchers at 11.30 o'clock.
N.B. – The Ambulance is Not Available.

ARM AMPUTATION IN MID-AIR

A.E. Harrison

In 1922 Mr A.E. Harrison, Honorary Secretary of the Glamorgan Branch, sent the following article to the Red Cross Journal. *It concerns a remarkable operation that took place in mid-air, without proper medical instruments, at a Cardiff tramway depot.*

'AN EMPLOYEE WAS DRAGGED by the arm 35ft from the ground, where his arm became locked in the cog-wheels of an elevator. The gentleman in charge of the depot was Commandant Preston of the BRCS. He reached the man and found that the only way to release him and save his life was to amputate the arm.

'The doctor had not arrived, and as every minute was vital, the Commandant took it upon himself to conduct the operation whilst the victim was suspended in the air by his arm. Mr Preston applied a tourniquet over the brachial artery and amputated the limb with his pocket knife.

'The man was then lowered in an improvised stretcher to the ground and taken to the King Edward VII Hospital, where he made a rapid recovery.

'In acknowledging with thanks a letter of appreciation from Sir Arthur Stanley, Chairman of Red Cross National Council, Commandant Preston said: "I only did what I have trained myself to do as a member of the British Red Cross Society – to use my resourcefulness in an emergency." '

1. King George VI and Queen Elizabeth inspecting a Red Cross motor convoy leaving for France during World War II

2. The signing of the first Geneva Convention, 1864

3. Henry Dunant - 'father of the Red Cross'

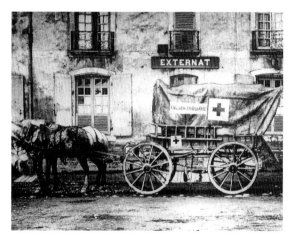

4. The Woolwich Ambulance, Franco-Prussian War, 1870–71

5. The steam launch *Queen Victoria* transporting sick and wounded troops in support of the Medical Services on the Nile, 1884

6. Ambulances in action, South African War, 1899–1902

7. The first purpose-built British hospital train, South African War

8. A dressing station, Abbeville, France 1915, World War I

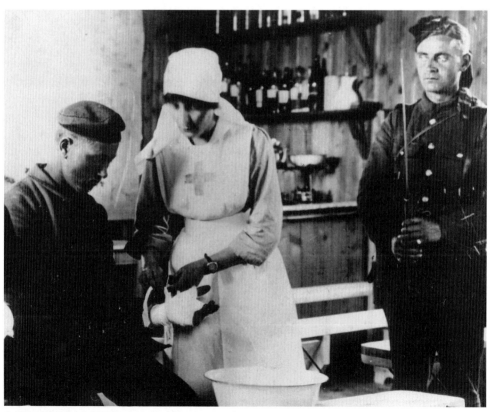

9. World War I VAD dressing the hand of a wounded German Soldier

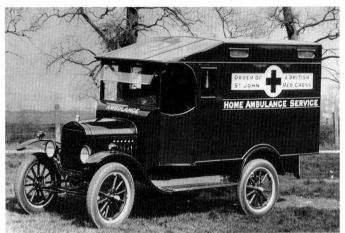

10. A Peacetime
ambulance of the Home
Ambulance Service, 1921

11. Children at
the Hackney &
Stoke Newington
Clinic getting
ultraviolet ray
treatment, 1928

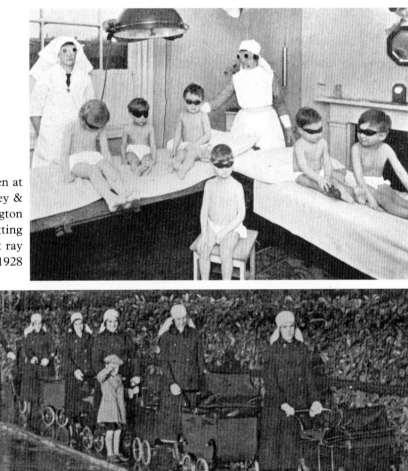

12. Pram Parade from the Infant Welfare Centre, Amersham, Bucks, 1933

13. A tableau representing Cancer Research in Plymouth, National Health Week, 1923

14. Surrey VAD detachment building their own garage, 1930s

15. First Aid station on the Bath Road with Berkshire VADs, 1930

16. Red Cross Food Parcel Day –
An Oflag scene in Germany,
World War II

17. The ICRC ship *VEGA* carrying food to the Channel Islands, 1944

18. VADs on an Air Raid
Training exercise, circa
1939

DRIVING IN THE GENERAL STRIKE

The following is an account (by one L.J.F.) of the help he* gave as a Red Cross volunteer during the General Strike of 1926. It first appeared in the June 1926 edition of The Auto.

ALREADY, STORIES OF THE GREAT STRIKE are becoming as unfashionable as were tales of the Great War by the year 1920. But since nothing about it seems yet to have appeared in print, some light mention of the work of those motorists who volunteered for duty with the Red Cross in London during the nine days may not be quite out of place.

Personally, I have always been rather vague about the Red Cross in peacetime, well enough as one knew it in the war. At hill climbs, when hill climbs were, one used to see the St John's men with their ambulance, but I doubt if I ever connected them with the organisation that has its headquarters in Berkeley Street. However, there they belong and the Joint Council of the Order of St John of Jerusalem in England and the British Red Cross Society –a fine title, that – seem to direct from the same address all the business of voluntary ambulance work throughout the country. On the off-chance of a job I rang them up when the strike came and, having been none too lucky in my efforts elsewhere, I was delighted when I found that I could really have something to do. For the rest of the 'duration' I led, as a matter of fact, quite a strenuous life, but I need not recount merely personal adventures here.

The job of work that the Red Cross found for itself – or rather, I believe, had

---

* It's more likely to have been a "he" – men drove buses etc in the General Strike.

allotted to it by the Government – for the strike period was, *inter alia*, to provide transport for the movement of patients to and from hospitals. The London County Council continued to look after casualties, but to deal with the out-patients and others the Red Cross formed a transport column composed of private cars, loaned and in most cases driven by their owners.

The response to the appeal made from Headquarters was an excellent one and – though there were one or two narrow escapes on busy days – a sufficient number of cars was always available to meet the needs of the hospitals. And the drivers 'stuck it' magnificently. Duty of this kind inevitably involves a great deal of standing by and, though there are worse ways of spending an afternoon than sitting in one's car in Berkeley Street reading a novel, that kind of thing is apt to become boring; however, one heard but few grumbles. Again, and particularly to the woman driver, the work itself must have been more than a little trying. There is nothing more tiring than continual driving in traffic, while the exploration of the back streets of Poplar in search of an elusive patient was not, perhaps, an invariably pleasant experience. However, the same good people came, day after day, did their jobs up to time and were always cheery over them.

It was not a big affair, as affairs went during the strike, this carrying off rather over a thousand poor souls, who would otherwise have had to whistle for hospital or home, as the case might be. Still, it was very much a job worth the doing and it has left behind it some rather pleasant memories.

WORLD WAR II

Storm Clouds Gather

Throughout 1938 both the nation and the Red Cross prepared for the possibility of war.

In the aftermath of the Munich crisis, a letter from the Home Secretary to Dame Beryl Oliver, in charge of the VAD Department at National Headquarters, illustrates the shared concerns.

5th October, 1938.

Dear Dame Beryl Oliver

        I should like to express to you my deep appreciation of the help that the British Red Cross Society gave us during the recent difficult weeks.

        By putting your organisation and your personnel so freely at the disposal both of the Home Office and of the Local Authorities, you gave us a reassurance that if the need had arisen a first aid system would have been brought swiftly into existence.

Yours sincerely
Samuel Hoare

ESCAPE FROM FRANCE, 1940

Monica Smythe

The following extract is taken from a letter by Monica Smythe, mother of the Olympic show-jumper, Pat Smythe, to the Red Cross Journal *in 1940. In it Mrs Smythe describes the gruelling journey she and her invalid husband had to undertake across France when German forces occupied the country.*

THANKS TO A SERIES OF REAL MIRACLES and hair-breadth escapes, here we are safely in England, and the feeling of comparative security leaves me almost stunned. What we have been through would have been difficult enough with a strong and fit person, so you can imagine the anxiety one has experienced travelling with an invalid, whose courage, however, was an example to all around him. We met with nothing but friendliness and generosity from the French people, as well as great praise for the morale of our soldiers and the marvellous feats of our RAF.

Above all I am writing to tell you that it was largely through my Red Cross uniform (which I had fortunately decided to take, although it meant travelling with an extra suitcase), that we are here now, and must tell you a few experiences to show how the good old Red Cross inspires confidence.

To my great inward anxiety, we were considerably delayed from leaving Aix en Provence. The local police had made a mistake over my passport, and had sent it away. I bicycled thirty kilometres in a thunderstorm, got past two armed guard forts, and found it at the Prefecture at Chambery, just as the officials were sending the envelope to England! A precious twenty-four hours was lost at Lyons, with Italian planes over the town, as my husband was too 'done in' to travel on. Then I got him on to the only train for Bordeaux. It was filled to the roof, with refugees of every description. We never moved out of the crammed railway carriage for forty-four hours, and knew what thirst and hunger meant.

It was quite impossible to move or get down the corridor to the 'toilette' for two days and nights. On the second day we got water through the window from Boy Scouts and the French Red Cross. The most pathetic thing of all, I think, was when our train was drawing up in a siding, where French soldiers were lying on straw. They came and looked in at us, and without speaking a word, went off, returning soon with their rations in their caps, and handed them to us.

When we reached Bordeaux, we heard with shock of the Armistice possibility. A kind Frenchman, with a car, took us, seeing how sick my husband looked, into Bordeaux, to the Consulate. You may have read descriptions of Bordeaux; the streets lined several deep, with cars and carts piled high with household goods, mattresses, luggage, etc. You could not walk on the pavements or get any food whatever.

At the Consulate we were told to get out to Le Verdon at once if we wanted to leave France. This was the harbour at the mouth of the estuary, eighty miles away. There was a boat leaving in a few hours, 'But,' said they, 'unless you have a private car, you have no hope, there is not a car or taxi for hire in the whole of Bordeaux.'

My husband looked 'all in' and could not walk another step, and we stood in the 'Grande Place' (at the Consulate I had changed into my uniform for the first time since leaving England) among thousands of others wanting transport. German planes swooped down on us, and each time I felt the under-carriage *must* hit our heads – it was terrifying, but I felt furious! At that moment I saw two French Red Cross nurses and pushed my way over to them, showed them my husband, and explained that we were in dire need of a car. I can't tell you how good they were to us – they showed real sister feeling. They stroked my uniform and VAD 'Mobile' badge and said, with a sigh, 'Ah! Que c'est bien joli!' They were impressed too by Eric's Legion of Honour (he wore it in his buttonhole, like all Frenchmen do) and also with his alarming appearance. After a few minutes one went off and returned *with a car* she had commandeered from the Red Cross for us.

We made the driver go like fury away from the threatened city – and at last saw sea and harbour ahead with many ships. As we drove into the mole, the driver pulled up, leapt out of the car and ran for his life. Overhead were German planes roaring, and we had driven right into it. Five bombs dropped in front of us and part of the jetty went up with a roar, all the children on the jetty were running too and hiding under cars, etc, shrieking and crying bitterly; several people were killed on the beach. I couldn't see any sort of solid building, and Eric's joints had 'seized up' completely. We had an awful job retrieving our driver, and I had visions of Eric threatening him with his stick until he consented to drive on to the end of the jetty, where the tender awaited us – the 'Madura', our ship, had had to move further out to sea because of the enemy bombing. Burly French sailors seized our suitcases and insisted on carrying Eric. The voice of the naval Captain-in-Charge sent a thrill through me as it was lovely meeting someone British again. Seeing the Red Cross uniform, he whispered in my ear – 'You can do so much to reassure the crowds on board.'

The ship, a British–India boat, which normally carries 160 people, was full already, but the purser, when I threatened that Eric might not survive the voyage, managed to give him a bunk – in fact, many of the regular passengers, well and hearty, turned out of their cabins for sick refugees in the most noble spirit. I put him straight to bed. Then I put on indoor uniform and reported for duty.

For the first day out we were not escorted and there was no convoy. After that we could see two British destroyers in the distance. But the horror to me was the hundreds and hundreds of babies and children on board, and how to save them. We were five times chased by submarines. We had life-saving equipment for 200 and we were 1,666 on board – quite incredible. There were over 250 babies under two years old, beginning from three weeks old. Ten wounded were brought on board from Bordeaux Hospital.

There was no one to do a thing, so I undertook to do all I could, and really it was the most marvellous opportunity for service anyone could pray for, and from then on I never had a moment to think of bombs, submarines, etc, and could at the same time keep an eye on my own invalid, tucked in his bunk.

My chief problem was the hundreds of babies, due to no fresh fruit and much wrong feeding, etc, colic, constipation, etc, were rife, and it was a great moment when I found the barber's shop had one bottle of liquid paraffin. There were bad ears from the noise, and everything from sea sickness (in a comparatively calm Bay of Biscay) upwards. I only had to appear on deck in uniform to be pounced upon – 'I want the Red Cross nurse. Please will you come and see my sick wife and child?'

Oh! the joy of sighting Cornwall's coastline, and also when three Curtis fighters roared overhead in the Channel. All the time we were aboard, we never saw any planes that were not German or Italian – the latter not so alarming.

At Falmouth, the doctor himself examining us took my husband and me home, and put us up, seeing Eric's state of health.

We have seen war and its horrors, and the collapse of France. We know that morale is half the battle, from leaders downwards. This is what will carry us through the very unpleasant time which lies ahead.

ADVENTURES OF A
NAVAL VAD

Helen Long

Helen Long is a freelance writer who has contributed articles to the national press and written several books about World War II. This contribution has been adapted from her book Change into Uniform *(1978).*

A BUFF ENVELOPE CONTAINED THE FOLLOWING SUMMONS: 'Priority . . . You are to report to Haslar Hospital Gosport on Monday November 11th (1940).'

'Vasco, you're late!' Miss Waistell said, as I rushed headlong down into RN Hospital Haslar's massive cellars in the middle of an air-raid. 'No doubt you were delayed,' she continued, completely disregarding the perilous journey I'd had from non-functioning Waterloo to bomb-ridden Portsmouth Harbour Station. 'You will have to learn that here navy time is five minutes before time.'

On my way to 'join up', I had scrambled aboard the hospital's pinnace [light sailing boat] for the crossing from Portsmouth Harbour to Haslar's jetty as fires lit the skies on both sides of the water. Our skipper dropped anchor halfway across and we sat, blacked out, and waited for the gunfire to die down. The gently lapping water against the small, stationary boat contrasted oddly with the stabbing searchlight fingers that probed the sky and converged on specks of enemy planes.

'There's a double red on at Haslar,' the coxswain warned us, 'so you'd best get straight down to the cellars, and if you girls'll hop off quick, I'll not tie up here at all.' So saying, he used his boat-hook to hold us close alongside an open cutter which was obviously to serve us as a bridge. I found it astonishing that, lying side by side, the gunwales of those two boats managed never to rise and fall in unison as we clambered ashore in an ungainly fashion, clutching our cases.

A rating returning to HMS *Hornet* shouldered our bags to the impressive hospital gates, and the Regulating Petty Officer who checked us in shouted at us to make a dash for the cellars – 'Over there, nurse.' So, instantly, I was a naval nurse, and within Haslar's maze of cellars came face to face for the unforgettable first time with 'Madam'.

Miss Waistell was the Red Cross Commandant in charge of all VADs at Haslar and universally known as Madam. She was responsible for some 220 girls, for 'girls' to her we all most certainly were: hers to protect, chasten, discipline, cherish and fight for.

Up the linoleum-covered, brass-nosed stairs in 'D Block' she dominated her office, the nerve-centre from which she prosecuted her own particular war. On the wall opposite her littered desk a large map of the world was liberally bespattered with small Red Cross flags in greater or lesser density. Each represented one of her girls, be she serving at sea, in a naval hospital, or in the sick bay of a shore establishment at home or overseas. With a flourish of her uniformed arm she would indicate a healthy growth of diminutive flags in Londonderry, Colombo, Trincomalee, Simonstown, Durban, Port Said, Alexandria, Cairo, Brisbane, Melbourne, Adelaide and Bombay. But she always stressed the equally important, if not *more* important, work being done by her girls at home in less glamorous surroundings.

Madam had a stentorian voice, a masculine gait, wore her uniform with authority and was beloved by us all. Her loyalty to us was matched only by her loyalty to Haslar, and she would not hesitate to tackle the Surgeon Rear Admiral on our behalf.

'I've told the girls in the galley to keep your suppers hot,' she went on. 'So as soon as the Double Red is over you can get it upstairs. Vasco [she never *did* get my name right], I believe that my-brother-the-Admiral knew your father in the last war. I think it was your father who saved his life by taking his leg off at Bighi Hospital in Malta.' This disturbing piece of information, vouchsafed by the light of a hurricane lamp as the all-clear sounded, established an immediate and happy bond between us.

In 1946, with Victory in Europe and the Far East behind us, we girls were becoming restive and could no longer envisage what we were doing as our war effort. Responding to our frustration, Madam initiated some improvements for us. We were to be allowed ashore in civilian clothes and so got away with wearing make-up and higher heels.

Soon we were to be released, and preparing for our departure, realised how well the navy had cared for its own. Substantially fed and housed, we had travelled the world at their Lordships' behest. I had spent over two years in Egypt and had circumnavigated the continent of Africa, being mightily convoy-protected on the high seas. We had been kept in good health and granted generous leaves with travel warrants. Courtesy of the British Red Cross Society, promotion and seniority had come our way and we had been drafted at suitable intervals. It had been a civilised way of living and had commended itself to most of us, most of the time.

Checked out medically, issued with civilian clothing coupons, and with documents signed, we had received a few ribbons and medals to add to our small collections. It was all over and it was too much to bear. I found myself dawdling at the last moment, blowing my nose and making hasty repairs to my face.

Madam was stomping up and down the corridor in her sensible shoes, her feet turned elegantly out at ten-to-two, her wise old eyes overbright. It was time that we were gone. 'Now come along all you girls,' I could hear her saying – she who had always been there to see us off on foreign tours or other drafts with advice about being sure to take topees for the tropics or navy-blue bloomers for ships' companionways.

No doubt, I thought, as we crowded around her, shaking her warmly by the hand that had often made us cups of cocoa late at night, some *had* been disappointed or disillusioned by their years in the Service. For myself, I knew that I would *never* regret having spent five and a half years of my youth as a naval Red Cross VAD in wartime.

A TASTE OF HOME

The following reminiscences are taken from letters written by former POWs in response to a request for recollections of the Red Cross during World War II.

T. Marshall – Newport, Gwent

It starts back in June 1942, when I was serving in the old 8th Army in North Africa, fighting against Rommel's armies. On 21 June I was taken prisoner with about 5,000 others. We were taken to a POW camp outside Benghazi, and then eventually to Rimini in Italy. We were a sorry lot when we arrived at this camp. Most of us were suffering some complaint or other – bugs, lice, dysentery, wounds and, by now, malnutrition.

Most of us hadn't heard of the Red Cross or St John before the war, but in a matter of days we were receiving medical aid parcels. We cleaned out an old building and set up a hospital with our own medical orderlies.

As the weeks went by, all the men rapidly lost weight because the food rations were so stingy. Then one day, as my friend and I were walking around the compound, a shout went up: 'Red Cross food parcels have arrived.' Everyone rushed to the barbed wire fence in front of the Italian Office – anyone in the way would have been knocked over! After the parcels were inspected and counted by our officer, we were told to form ourselves into groups of seven because there weren't enough parcels to go round.

On parcel-issue day the Italian officer would open the parcels for inspection and stab a hole in the tinned food. This was to stop prisoners from hoarding food to escape. Sometimes the tins would explode, covering the officer and the guards with smelly food (laughter from the British)!

Among the contents of the parcels were packets of tea, sugar and dried milk, so of course the old English habit of brewing up started. Everybody now looked for wood to make a fire, and the first items to go were the wooden boards of our bunk beds. My mate Charlie and I, being on the bottom bunk, were soon sleeping on the floor. We used to take it in turns to collect wood chippings that came flying over the wire fence as the Italian men chopped wood for their fires . . .

Eventually we moved to another camp near Milan, where we worked in the fields. Come October, when Italy capitulated, 15 of us comrades escaped into Switzerland. Yet again I met up with the Red Cross, who delivered me another two food parcels sent from home!

I never pass a Red Cross box without putting something in it.

S.W.R. Kent – Edenbridge, Kent

. . . Food parcels gave us the will to live.

Alex Robinson – Tunbridge Wells, Kent

The German food rations consisted of a few potatoes boiled in their jackets, a cupful of cabbage soup, three or four slices of black bread with a small portion of margarine. In addition, about once a week we had a spoonful of jam or a ration of cheese or fish. At no time in my two years as a POW did I see an egg or any milk. It was extremely difficult to survive on these rations and as a result thousands of Russian POWs died of malnutrition.

W.H. Slocombe – Corsham, Wiltshire

. . . The camp rations were not enough to keep a cat alive.

W.J. Gard – Barnstaple, Devon

Copied from the camp notice board and taken from the Scottish POW magazine: 'Over 5½ million parcels were packed and dispatched by the British Red Cross during 1942. In addition, heavy consignments of boots, medical comforts, games and musical instruments were sent to camps. The weekly output from Red Cross packing centres in the British Isles is 140,000 parcels. Of this, 15,000 are passed for Indian POWs, the cost being met by the Indian Red Cross.

The latest report shows that there are now 16,000 POWs whose next of kin are resident in Scotland.

Scottish Red Cross are dispatching 20,000 food parcels a week.

Eric Frais – Middlesbrough, Cleveland

I was in a Dulag Luft prisoner-of-war camp. About the end of 1944, two of us in our hut began to suffer bad stomach pains and could not eat anything. There was no medical officer either English or German in the camp. We were put into a makeshift hospital. After about two weeks having not been able to eat anything, we were both completely yellow. I think we were on our last legs and delirious.

Suddenly, a Luftwaffe officer and a doctor came in, and in English the doctor said, 'You have got severe jaundice. Get a message to your fellow POWs – tell them to bring all the dried fruit from the Red Cross parcels because fruit is the only thing you can take. I will tell an orderly to prepare a fruit stew which you will digest.'

This was done and gradually we regained our strength. Thanks to the food parcels our lives were saved.

Edwin Stonard – Stevenage, Hertfordshire

. . . The only subject that aroused any excitement was the slightest rumour that Red Cross parcels were in the vicinity. Those oblong boxes with a large red cross on the outside and the printed words 'Gift of the Red Cross and St John' would raise the hopes of the most despondent!

. . . The main source of information on prisoners of war came from the International Red Cross HQ in Geneva. They obtained their information by visiting camps, questioning POWs and also sending cards asking for details and confirmation of those men who were missing or killed. All the information was then relayed to the various organisations who requested it. It was to be lamented that these facilities were not carried out for POWs in the Far East.*

. . . I was reported missing in action and no news of my whereabouts was known for many months. The Red Cross gave support to my family and to all the wives and mothers at home who sought comfort during the anxious time of waiting for news.

E. Carter – Solihull, W. Midlands

. . . In 1940 I was in Stalag VIII B when I met a friend who was waiting to go home for he was badly wounded. He had just received his first food parcel and he made me a thing called a blower. It was not very big, consisting of a winder

---

* Japan had not ratified the 1929 Geneva Convention on prisoners of war.

that turned a small fan, but it was very useful. It was used to make a draught through a small tunnel into a fireplace, which meant that you were able to cook your food and brew a cup of char with the minimum of fuel. Who invented it nobody knew, but when you moved, your blower went with you.

. . . Tea leaves had more lives than a cat. First they were used to make tea – again and again until they were white. Then you dried them and smoked them!

A.L. Parker – Mablethorpe, Lincolnshire

We were getting a regular issue of Red Cross parcels and they were great morale boosters. One day a POW went missing and the guards kept the rest of us out on parade for some time while a search was made for him. In spite of the discomfort to ourselves, everyone said what a good fellow he was to have escaped and we hoped he'd make it.

Attitudes soon changed, however, when, after a few days, he was discovered in the Red Cross Store, where he had been eating his way through our food parcels. He quickly became the most unpopular man in the camp as interference with the parcel issue was regarded as a major disaster.

John Airey – Garston, Liverpool

I was serving with No. 3 Commando and was captured at Merville in 1944 while attacking coastal batteries. After travelling across war-torn Europe, I found myself at a German *stalag* on the German–Polish Border. We were ordered to work in a local sugar factory for 12 hours a day, 16 hours on Sundays. Our daily rations were a bowl of soup and one-fifth of a loaf of bread. As I look back, it doesn't seem credible that we existed on such meagre rations, but we were thankful to be alive. Working alongside us at the factory were Polish girls and older women, who, after the Warsaw uprising, were transported at a moment's notice from their homes to work for the Germans. It was heartbreaking to see them trudging to work through the snow with only old sacks for protection against the icy wind. But they made light of their hardships, instead pitying us and never complaining of their own plight.

On Christmas Day we were to receive Red Cross parcels – one to every five prisoners. Imagine the excitement and eagerness we felt when Christmas Day actually arrived! Here was this parcel containing lots of good things – tea, cocoa, chocolate, tinned meats, tinned milk, butter, jam – all ready for eating.

Then we thought of those poor Polish families almost starving. Somehow, the thought of having this marvellous parcel all to ourselves was unthinkable, so four friends and I spontaneously decided that we would give the parcel to a Polish family, keeping just a packet of tea for ourselves.

I cannot put into words the joy and thankfulness on the faces of that Polish family when we gave them our parcel; nor can I explain how, when we drank our tea and ate our bread it tasted like manna from heaven.

Strange as it may seem, although I have had many happy Christmases with family and friends since, none will ever give me a greater sense of the true spirit of Christmas than the day in 1944 when I shared my Christmas in Poland with that Polish family.

'Mrs Churchill's Fund'

The Lady Soames, DBE

Recalling her mother, Clementine Churchill's, valuable role as Chairman of the Red Cross Aid to Russia Appeal, Lady Soames draws on her own recollections, the records of the time and the booklet, My Journey to Russia, *written by her mother in 1945.*

W HEN GERMANY ATTACKED RUSSIA IN 1941, Winston Churchill, despite his lifelong hostility to communism, at once declared Great Britain's determination to ally itself with the Soviet Union in her ferocious struggle against the Nazi invaders. As German troops advanced into the heartland of Russia, the Russian people were filled with admiration for their own army's valiant defence of their homeland. It was a long and gruelling struggle, which brought appalling hardship to the people. News of their suffering aroused a wave of sympathy throughout Britain, and there was a general, spontaneous desire to organise help and relief for the new ally.

Various proposals to raise funds were canvassed; in particular, action was taken by the Red Cross and St John War Organisation in association with the Women's Voluntary Services (WVS) to collect and send warm clothing to Russia for women and children. The overall priority, however, was for medical and surgical supplies. It soon became clear that the scale of Russian needs and the difficulties of procuring and delivering them called for a coordinated national effort.

On learning from Moscow that Soviet authorities would welcome funds and would send a list of their most urgent requirements, the Red Cross and St John War Organisation decided to launch a national appeal and set up a special committee. Sir Philip Chetwode, Chairman of the Executive Committee of the War Organisation, invited Clementine Churchill to become Chairman of the Red Cross Aid to Russia Appeal. She at once accepted this new and onerous addition to her obligations as wife of the Prime Minister and her already considerable war work. She was deeply moved by the sufferings of the Russian people and accurately gauged the strength of sympathy for the Russian cause in this country. She also saw that a national effort to send help and relief was a great opportunity to show in a practical way the very real desire of the country to render what help it could to Russia. Her twin roles as wife of the Prime Minister and head of the appeal also demonstrated that the British Government was at one with feelings in the country.

The Red Cross Aid to Russia Fund was launched in mid-October 1941 and the response was immediate: contributions flowed in from all over the country, from rich and poor alike. Administration of the fund was admirably organised by the War Organisation and just before Christmas, Clementine Churchill was able to broadcast the almost incredible news that the fund had already passed the £1 million mark, its original target.

Fund-raising continued apace. Throughout the country local Aid to Russia committees were formed. Towns and cities held flag days and organised Anglo-Soviet Weeks. Auctions and theatrical galas took place, and school-children and office workers all raised money on a regular basis. In 1943 £12,500 was raised at the England v. Wales football match, the largest sum ever raised for charity by one sporting event. A large source of continuous income came from the Red Cross Penny-a-Week Fund, which was strongly supported by industrial workers.

There is no doubt that the leadership of Clementine Churchill helped focus national enthusiasm for the cause, but she was much more than a figurehead. Despite other calls on her time, she immersed herself in the appeal, working closely with the committee and making herself thoroughly knowledgeable about the supplies and means of delivery required. She worked particularly closely with Mabel Johnson, secretary to the committee, who also became a great friend.

Even before the Aid to Russia Committee was set up, it was clear that the scale of the Russian requirements and the effectiveness of our response to them would be beyond the powers of even an experienced organisation like the Joint War Organisation; full Government cooperation was essential. It was therefore proposed that the Ministry of Supply should undertake the necessary purchasing for the Aid to Russia Fund, advised by an expert committee representing such organisations as the Trades Union Congress and the Mineworkers' Federation – bodies which had an interest in providing medical aid to Russia on a large scale.

It was a vast operation. Procuring supplies was the first step, and it was necessary to introduce special methods of production to meet some of the Russian demands. Then the goods and equipment had to be packed and conveyed to Russia, which meant overcoming the difficulties of wartime transport and ignoring the dangers to convoys. At times the Soviet representatives expressed disappointment at the slowness of deliveries: the urgency of their own needs made them overlook the problems faced by their allies, such as the scarcity of raw materials and the immense quantities involved, which combined to make the delivery of goods to the USSR such a complex operation.

Lists were issued regularly to inform the public of the total supplies sent. By October 1942, 11 months after the appeal's launch, 18 consignments had been shipped to the Soviet Union. In addition to portable X-ray units and ambulances, supplies included clothing, bedding, drugs and a large range of surgical instruments. A single delivery of 63,000 hot water bottles and 523,000 yards of rubber sheeting gives some idea of the scale of the operation.

A number of other, politically motivated, organisations also established funds for helping Russia, but none of these agencies caught the imagination of the public as much as 'Mrs Churchill's Fund'. The Red Cross Aid to Russia Fund was apolitical, allowing people to respond purely on a humanitarian basis. However, there was no doubt that the name of Churchill, combined with the respect and confidence inspired by Clementine Churchill herself, fired the enthusiasm of people throughout the country.

Towards the end of 1944, Clementine Churchill was invited by the Soviet government and the Soviet Red Cross to visit the USSR, an invitation she warmly accepted. Although she had worked for the Red Cross continuously for four years she had not, up to this point, been a 'uniformed member'; now it seemed best that, for the purposes of this journey, she should wear uniform. She was accordingly appointed a Vice President of the County of London Branch of the British Red Cross Society.

Clementine Churchill arrived in Moscow on 2 April 1945 accompanied by her own private secretary, Grace Hamblin, and by Mabel Johnson (Secretary to the fund). The central purpose of their visit was to arrange for the equipment of two hospitals at Rostov-on-Don, which would stand as a lasting memorial to the Red Cross Aid to Russia Fund. But the medical aid supplied by the fund had been used in many areas, which gave the English party the opportunity to visit a large number of war zones. Their travels took them to Leningrad, Stalingrad, towns and cities in the Caucasus, Sebastopol, Yalta and other places in the Crimea, plus Odessa and Kursk. The Soviet government provided a special train for the journey and they were accompanied by several high-ranking officials, who acted as their hosts and facilitated all the arrangements.

During these days Clementine was constantly in touch with the British Ambassador and his staff. Through the embassy she received messages from Winston. On 2 April he cabled: 'Lovely accounts of your speech and reception received here. At the moment you are the one bright spot in Anglo-Russian relations.'

Winston also told Clementine that the Ambassador would show her the Foreign Office telegrams, which spelt out the current grave difficulties between the British and Soviet governments. In a cable on 6 April, Winston told her: 'Please speak always of my earnest desire for continuing friendship of British and Russian peoples and of my resolve to work for it perseveringly. . . .' So, when Clementine had a private interview with Mr Molotov, and she and Mabel Johnson were later received by Marshal Stalin, she knew the background to the lethal political tensions.

Clementine and her party spent two or three days in the major cities, visiting Stalingrad two years after the horror of its six-month siege. She saw the vast rebuilding operations which were in progress but was aghast at the sight of the ravaged city. She later wrote: '. . . My first thought was, how like the centre of Coventry or the devastation around St Paul's, except that here the havoc and obliteration seem to spread endlessly. . . . The imagination is baffled by the attempt to encompass calamity on so vast a scale.'

The focal point of their visit was Rostov-on-Don, where the Aid to Russia Fund was undertaking the complete re-equipment of two large hospitals which had suffered severe damage. The original intention had been to equip 500 beds in each, but when they saw the scale of the needs, it was decided to increase the number to 1,500 beds. This on-the-spot revision of plans highlighted the practical value of Clementine Churchill's visit, quite apart from the goodwill engendered.

The party had earlier heard (from Mr Molotov himself) of the death of President Roosevelt, the shock and sorrow of which was felt also by their hosts. But deep in Russia, where news from the outer world scarcely penetrated, only echoes of the great events now rolling to their climax thousands of miles away in Western Europe reached Clementine and her companions. Winston had warned her that once she left Moscow and was out of touch with the embassy, any secret communications must cease, and that cables would be *en clair*. But from telegrams her husband sent they learned of the forward surge of liberating armies, the execution of Mussolini, the surrender of German forces in Italy, and how, on 30 April, Hitler had shot himself in the air-raid bunker of the Chancellery in Berlin.

Although deeply engrossed by her daily programme, Clementine now yearned to be at home and at Winston's side; but her task in Russia was not yet completed, and it was not until 5 May that she and her party arrived back in Moscow. Now she could receive fuller news, and in a private cable to her on 4 May, Winston confided: '. . . You seem to have had a triumphant tour and I only wish matters would be settled between you and the Russian common people. However, there are many other aspects of this problem than those you have seen on the spot . . .' He then gave her a brief synopsis of the victorious events which had taken place in her absence, continuing: '. . . and we are all occupied here with preparations for Victory – European Day. . . . I need scarcely tell you that beneath these triumphs lie poisonous politics and deadly international rivalries. Therefore you should come home after rendering the fullest compliments to your hospitable hosts. . . .'

Clementine, although longing to set out for home, had several more commitments to fulfil. One engagement took her and Mabel Johnson to the Kremlin, where they received at the hands of the First Vice Chairman of the Supreme Soviet of the USSR the Order of the Red Banner of Labour and the Medal of Labour respectively, awarded to them by Marshal Stalin. And at a luncheon given by the Soviet government two days before their departure, Mrs Molotov presented Clementine with a beautiful diamond ring as a token of 'eternal friendship'.

The party did not leave for home until 11 May, so they were in Moscow for VE Day on 8 May. Clementine's thoughts were with Winston, and early that morning she cabled him: 'All my thoughts are with you on this supreme day, my darling. It could not have happened without you.'

A religious service was hastily arranged and held at the British Embassy, and in the afternoon Clementine listened to Winston's broadcast from London. On the evening of 9 May, Clementine broadcast a message on Moscow radio from Prime Minister Churchill to Marshal Stalin: 'It is my firm belief that on the friendship and understanding between the British and Russian peoples depends the future of mankind.'

On 11 May, the morning of her departure, Mrs Churchill wrote a letter in her own hand to Marshal Stalin:

> My dear Marshal Stalin,
>   I am leaving your great country after a wonderful & unforget-
> table visit.
>   I have seen with sorrow some of the ravages caused by a wicked

and ruthless Enemy and observed the dignity, courage and patience of your people.

I have enjoyed the most warm-hearted hospitality & everywhere I have been welcomed with the greatest kindness and enthusiasm. And my happiness has been crowned by being received by you & by the decorations which you have bestowed upon Miss Johnson and myself.

I know of the international difficulties which have not been surmounted, but I know also of my Husband's resolve and confidence that a complete understanding between the English-Speaking World and the Soviet Union will be achieved and maintained as this is the only hope of the World.

Yours sincerely,

Clementine S. Churchill

I count myself fortunate to have been in your country in these days of Victory, and to have seen the Sun of Peace rise in Moscow.

Soon after her return home, Clementine wrote a small booklet entitled *My Visit to Russia*. In it she described the journeyings she and her companions had made as emissaries of the British Red Cross and the warmth with which they were received. Reading it now with hindsight, one finds the oft-repeated expressions of friendship on either side ring somewhat hollow, for over 40 years of Cold War were to hold Europe and the West in their chill grip. But in reading Clementine Churchill's account, one must try to recapture the atmosphere of those days – the feelings of the British people who had been awestruck by the heroism and suffering of the Russians, and had found expression for them in their overwhelming support of the Red Cross Aid to Russia Fund. By 1947, although fund-raising had ceased in 1945, the Fund stood at £7,984,000.

In ending the account of her visit to Russia, Clementine wrote: 'I prayed as I turned to take my farewell look at Moscow, "May difficulties and misunderstandings pass, may Friendship remain".'

Writing as I do in 1994, these words have a ring of hope, indeed.

OCCUPATION OF THE CHANNEL ISLANDS

Pauline Samuelson

On 28 June 1940 the Germans bombed Guernsey and Jersey: 44 Channel Islanders were killed. Two days later the Islands were occupied, the only part of the British Isles to fall into enemy hands during World War II.

Earlier in the year, as first Norway, then Holland and Belgium were invaded, people on the larger Islands began to fear the worst. Many families, particularly those with children, chose to leave for the mainland of Britain. For families divided by war, the Red Cross Message Service was the only means of communication during the whole occupation. In Jersey it was called the Bailiff's Enquiry and News Office, while in Guernsey it was known as the Red Cross Message Bureau.

Leonie Trouteaud, the Guernsey administrator of the Message Service, gives us some vivid pictures of the occupation: 'In February 1941, six months after the occupation began, I had a call from the German headquarters informing me that a batch of messages had arrived. With great anticipation, I went to collect them on my bicycle. Imagine my consternation when I found that I had to sit in an office and count them with two soldiers standing beside me! There were 1,900 messages, each in a blue envelope. The box was too heavy to carry on my bicycle and therefore I had the doubtful pleasure of having to walk beside a German soldier whilst he pushed my bike carrying the box.'

Known to the Germans as the 'Red Cross Aunty', Miss Trouteaud went to the German headquarters each morning to collect the urgent messages of births and deaths. She then organised immediate delivery of them through her band of volunteers.

In the early days the Channel Islanders tried sending cryptic messages based on biblical quotations. This ploy was soon discovered and doubtful messages were confiscated. One day Miss Trouteaud was sent for and asked to explain a message: 'No more Sea Breezes'. She said that she had no idea what it meant but suggested that perhaps the sender was trying to convey the fact that nobody was allowed near the coast. The German officer-in-charge demanded that she send for the person responsible. A worried-looking woman later arrived to explain that she simply wanted to tell her sister on the mainland that their home, 'Sea Breezes', had been destroyed.

By the second year of the occupation, the Message Service had dealt with tens of thousands of messages on both of the larger islands, and there was no shortage of volunteers to help each day in sorting them out. Both incoming and outgoing messages were routed through the International Red Cross Central Tracing Bureau in Geneva. There, each form was checked by Red Cross workers to make sure it kept within the 25-word limit and infringed no news restrictions. The messages were then sorted by country of destination. Messages for families in the Channel Islands first went to the German Red Cross in Berlin; from there they travelled to the French Commission for the German Red Cross in Paris; finally they went to the Feld Kommandantur in the Channel Islands. The whole procedure could take up to four months, which must have seemed an eternity to those anxious for news, yet people today still remember with gratitude the pleasure those precious messages gave to lonely children and families torn apart by conflict.

After the D-Day landings of June 1944, the Channel Islands went through their worst period of the whole occupation. Vital supply links, which until then had gone through France, were severed and the German Occupying Force was unable to send fuel, food or medical supplies to the Islands. The civilian population was desperately hard hit. The position was horribly complicated: on one hand, as a result of the Normandy landings, Britain had regained control of all approaches to the Islands; on the other hand, the Islands were still under German control. The Bailiffs (elected officials) were thwarted in every attempt to approach the International Red Cross directly: they were only permitted to plead their case through the German Command. As winter set in and the siege continued, the situation deteriorated further. The Occupying Force began requisitioning more foodstuffs to feed its troops, and the soldiers themselves took to stealing chickens and pigs to supplement their meagre rations. Conditions, as described in the Islands' records, were 'verging on actual slow starvation'.

How long this stalemate could have continued is hard to judge. Fortunately for the islanders, it was broken in the late autumn of 1944, thanks partly to escapees from the larger islands spreading the word in England, and partly to the efforts of one Guernseyman, Major Ambrose Sherwill, who was the officer-in-charge of Channel Islands deportees interned in Germany. Through his close contact with the German Red Cross in the internment camp, the International Committee of the Red Cross (ICRC) was made aware of the terrible state of the civilian population on the Islands. At last the Bailiffs were able to go into action. At a meeting in November of that year they met representatives of the ICRC to discuss their relief needs. The subsequent arrival of the supply ship *Vega* was awaited with impatient excitement by the whole population.

Miss Trouteaud, administrator of the Red Cross Bureau in Guernsey, takes up the story: 'One morning in late 1944 Sanderführer Kraft told me that a Red Cross ship, the *Vega*, was due to arrive with food – "For you, you understand, not for us," as he put it. When the States (the Controlling Government Committee) informed us that this was to happen, we quickly set up a Red Cross and St John committee to discuss ways and means of unloading and distributing the food, clothing and medical supplies expected.

'On the evening of December 27th we went to the Plateau overlooking the harbour and saw the *Vega*, a splendid and moving sight. She was a lovely, slim white ship with a slender black and white funnel. On her bow from deck to water line was painted a large red cross on a white background. Amidships on a white background there was in large lettering "C INTERNATIONAL", standing for the International Committee of the Red Cross. She was flying the Swedish flag on her stern. Many people were there and all were weeping as we watched the ship move slowly into London Berth at the White Rock on the high tide. After five years of isolation, the ship seemed like something from outer space – it was a real contact with the outside world, and it seemed to us that she had arrived by some miracle.'

The *Vega* was unloaded by the Germans, as ordered by Red Cross representatives aboard the ship. Local people had to be present, however, at the unloading. The parcels – gifts from the New Zealand and Canadian Red Cross – were taken to a central hall and kept under constant guard. A smaller vessel was dispatched to Sark with supplies while the *Vega* travelled on to Jersey where the unloading process was repeated. Parcels were taken to selected shops, and each man, woman and child received one on production of their ration book. Special invalid parcels were distributed to the elderly and those suffering from TB or diabetes. The joy that people experienced from those first parcels is described by one recipient, who remembers 'having 1/4lb of tea in one hand and a bar of soap in the other – and not knowing which to do first – have a wash or make a cup of tea'.

The supply ship made six life-saving trips to the Channel Islands. In gratitude one family christened their baby Vega, while a stonemason in St

Helier, Jersey, expressed his feelings in Royal Square by carving the following inscription in the granite paving stones: VEGA + 1945.

The mercy ship is remembered by everyone in the Channel Islands who so nearly starved during the siege months. It remains a symbol of how the Red Cross came to the rescue when help was most needed during the long ordeal of German occupation.

THE BATTLE OF BRITAIN YEARS

Dame Anne Bryans, DBE

Dame Anne is one of the most distinguished members of the British Red Cross. Since she joined the Society in 1927 at the age of 18, she has held many senior appointments, both in peacetime and in war. Her Red Cross career has also led her into the wider spectrum of health care; she has been a trustee on several hospital boards and nursing school committees.

Working at the nerve centre of the Joint War Organisation of the Red Cross and St John in London, I witnessed the generosity that flowed in to support the British Red Cross during the darkest days of World War II. The Red Cross Societies of Canada, Australia, New Zealand, South Africa and India gave us great heart, and the wonderful support of the American Red Cross, who urged us, 'Ask for whatever you need and we will send it,' was a continual boost to our morale and our resources.

The Red Cross Societies of Holland, Poland, Norway and Czechoslovakia also had their headquarters in London, and early in the war a Franco-British committee was set up. A particular bonus was that the Belgian Red Cross was able to transmit information about missing men through Red Cross links in various foreign legations. Needless to say, we maintained daily contact with all these sister organisations.

The departments of the War Organisation were scattered around London in the great houses put at their disposal by generous owners. The importance of the Wounded, Missing and Prisoners of War Department was evident from the fact that King George lent the Lord Chamberlain's Office in St James's Palace to the Red Cross for the duration of the war.

As a member of the National Headquarters team, part of my particular job was to travel around the country visiting Branches and learning how members were coping with their mammoth wartime task. There was an upsurge in the demand for training, which sometimes had its lighter side – as this anecdote from a member illustrates.

> I remember at the beginning of the war how busy we Red Cross members were. We had all been trained in nursing and first aid and gave hours of our free time training in what was the beginning of Civil Defence. One exercise remains distinctly in my memory. We had a Mobile First Aid Unit, which consisted of a horse-box equipped with stretchers. We were called out one evening to a small village and it was a very dark night. Of course, we were not allowed light because of the black-out, and the 'casualties' were scattered all over the village. We were supposed to deal with them according to their injuries. Afterwards we assembled at the village hall for the usual comments and criticisms and it was realized that one of the 'casualties' was missing. We went out to find him as we had been told he was under the church wall. When we reached the wall, we found a note: 'Died of Exposure. Gone Home.'

After the evacuation of Dunkirk, Branches on the south coast were stretched to the limit providing support to the hospitals. The wounded poured in straight from the rescue ships. Beds were soon full and many stretchers lay on the floor. The theatre staff worked flat out and our VADs were magnificent. Trained only as Detachment members, they were unused to seeing horrendous wounds, gangrene and shattered limbs. They came off duty shocked and exhausted, but were always ready to go back on the next shift when it came.

In London I used a bicycle to travel round visiting the Medical Aid Posts which were organised in Tube stations. The stations were used as shelters by people who had been bombed out and by families who took to them at night because of their comparative safety and quiet – the London 'barrage' was continuous and terribly noisy. I shall never forget the sight of those people sleeping on the station platforms with only a blanket between them and the tracks.

In some shelters the Red Cross took complete charge of the Medical Aid Posts, and in others they were organised by Borough Authorities with Red

Cross and St John help. The shelters varied in size, the larger ones holding up to 3,000 people. They also varied in the 'comfort' they offered. Most had a water supply, electric light and occasional cooking facilities. Very few provided bunks, and sanitary arrangements were generally primitive to say the least. Some had separate sick bay areas used by the Medical Aid Posts and a nurse's 'office' that doubled as an examination room for the doctor.

Despite the primitive conditions, I seldom heard a grumble; in fact, I was more likely to hear, 'Oh well, there's always somebody worse off than me,' and this from the very people who had lost everything and suffered most. The shelterers became extremely attached to their temporary home and took grave exception to any changes introduced by the authorities. Often, we in the Red Cross found ourselves acting as mediators between them.

As I visited the shelters, I also felt enormous admiration for the VADs who sustained their voluntary effort night after night through all the bombing. Their duties ran from 5 p.m. until 7 a.m. which meant that they hardly saw daylight. In winter particularly, they had to travel through the black-out at both ends of their shift. Their working conditions were also far from ideal. Medical Aid Posts were constantly threatened by collapsing walls and falling debris from nearby bombs, and more than one Red Cross member was commended for the rescue work they undertook during the air raids of the blitz.

A VAD who had been posted to London from Cheshire wrote home giving an idea of his work:

> Ever since I arrived we've been having raids. Yesterday the Germans bombed us as we left Guy's Hospital in the Mobile Ambulances. We had to get under the car.
>
> . . . Tonight we've had a terrific raid with the guns roaring and bombs dropping. As I left the Tube and boarded a bus, a land mine fell out of the skies and put paid to the entrance of the Tube that I had just left.
>
> This is one of the largest shelters in London and we are very busy. At about 9 p.m. the doctor visits the shelter and I report any query cases. Tonight I reported on a little girl who was rushed off to hospital. The other day I had my first midwifery case and delivered a child about one in the morning and thoroughly enjoyed it. It was something that I had been dreading and yet when I was faced with it, I tackled it as if it was an everyday event in my life.
>
> The courage of the people is absolutely splendid; I never saw such brave people anywhere.

Another group of Red Cross workers I visited were those who ran Sick Bay Shelters in ordinary houses. The houses were obtained by the London Branch for the care of the homeless and those recovering from bomb injuries. An example of one such resident was Mr Sheppard, who lost his first home in Westminster, moved to Hendon and was bombed out a second time. Sleeping on the ground floor in his second home, he was completely buried by the fallen house and owed his life to the feather pillow on which he had been sleeping. When he tried to call for help he found he had lost his voice. Although only 45 years old, he looked like an old man of 70. He had no clothes and was brought to the sick bay wrapped in a blanket. Being very small, everything the staff put on him was far too big. The nurses shortened clothes to fit him and the amusement was great when it was discovered that the man was a tailor by trade. When he got his voice back his first words were to assure them that their work was perfect!

Wherever the Red Cross worked, by night or day (and many of us did hospital night duties after our daytime office jobs), our uniforms gave assurance and comfort. From the deepest Tube station to the air-raid shelter at the Savoy Hotel, where lots of elderly people took nightly refuge, we were able to fulfil our mission.

In 1940 the changed conditions of warfare meant that suffering was not restricted to armies in the field. The sick and the wounded were also ordinary people – the men, women and children at home. In so many bombed and devastated cities, like Coventry and Southampton, our VADs gave of their trained best. In London I was privileged to see the whole spectrum of Red Cross service – from international matters of world note to the individual care given by dedicated volunteers. All over Britain the spirit of that wartime service remains a lasting memory. For me it gives substance to the ideals on which the Red Cross Movement was founded.

INFANT DAYS AT CHANGI CAMP

Jenny Martin

THIS IS THE STORY of my first three and a half years, but even more, it is my mother's story. I have used her words and my own memories where possible.

'This is a nice time, lassie, to become pregnant,' said Dr Thompson a few days after the first air raid struck Singapore in December 1941.

In February 1942, along with about 500 other women, my mother was interned in Changi Prison in Singapore. The expected baby was due in July and eventually the time came to go into the Singapore Maternity Hospital, which had the Malay name of 'Kandang Kerbau' (Buffalo Pen). An Australian lady doctor, also an internee, accompanied her, and in the front of the car sat a Japanese soldier with rifle and fixed bayonet. With them went a young interpreter called Ishihara, who often tried to help the internees when he translated their requests to his Japanese superiors. He came to see my mother after I was born and said, 'You have a lovely daughter, Mrs Davidson. Can I do anything for you or take back a letter to the camp to your friends?'

'Ishihara,' my mother replied, 'you must be crazy. If the Kempetai found a letter of mine in your possession, you would risk the death penalty. No, please just tell them that you have seen me and the baby and that we are well.' He did this. Some time later he disappeared and we never knew what became of him.

My birth certificate gives the year of my birth as 2602 because it was calculated on the Buddhist calendar. I've always found this odd as the form was one left over from the colonial administration and is all in English!

Mother stayed in hospital for 14 days and an amah (children's nurse) helped with me until her return to Changi. Leong Kit Wan not only looked after me, she also persuaded the hospital cook to produce nourishing dishes for mother and smuggled them up to her. One day she said, 'All the pretty ladies on the roof think your baby very beautiful – prettiest baby in the hospital.' It turned out that after the European nurses were interned, their quarters were occupied by the Japanese 'comfort girls' brought to keep the military commanders happy. Perhaps they had never seen a baby with red hair before. When we left the hospital to go back to prison they all stood in line waving goodbye from their rooftop.

Back in the cells at Changi the August heat was terrific. Children cried, mothers lost their tempers, but I flourished and grew. Rations were short at first and grew shorter, so the occasional Red Cross parcel that got through was a big event. Mother was very thin, like all the other adults, and I often wonder if I got more than my share of food.

Christmas 1942, and a meeting was arranged with husbands and relatives from the military camp a few miles away. I was dressed up and wheeled out in my pram – a wooden Nestlé condensed milk box, lovingly converted by friends in the men's section of the prison. It was my first chance to see my father, but we were to be disappointed. As we turned slowly back to the prison, suddenly the Japanese commandant, Major-General Saito, appeared beside us. 'Never mind, lady,' he said. 'Something must have stopped your husband from getting here. I will arrange an Easter meeting.'

Thus it was on 10 March 1943 that I met my father. At Christmas he had been with a working party on an island looking after the Japanese officers' horses and the camp commandant had refused to let them attend the meeting. For the second time we stood in a long line with our backs to the prison wall, sentries standing in strategic positions. The men from the military camp were marched in and made to face our line. A whistle was blown and they rushed across the 20-yard gap. My father was there, very thin, under a huge Australian bush hat. As he picked me up, his first words to my mother were, 'Woman, don't you know you should never have a baby facing the sun?'

Father had made me a present – an old tin can filled with pebbles, attached to a stout wooden handle; it was a splendid rattle. Just before the whistle blew, Major-General Saito came over for a minute. 'I too have a baby daughter I have never seen. She is in Japan.'

At my first birthday an artist, Bill Charlton, painted an invitation scroll and all the children who came to the party signed it. Every mother dug into her small hoard of goodies and we had cakes of rice flour, banana fritters and peanut sweets.

On 6 May 1944 we were taken out of the prison and sent to an old RAF camp at Sime Road, where there was space to grow a few vegetables and room to run about in the open air. Here I started school. I had a few toys made from scraps of material and my favourite, Winnie the Pooh, who was sent in a parcel from the Netherlands to a child who screamed when she saw his funny yellow face, so he was given to me. I had books, too, including the *Changi Children's Christmas Book*, written and printed in the prison by some of the men.

Towards the end of 1944 there were rumours that the war would not last much longer, but it was not until 20 August 1945 that Liberator planes flew overhead dropping leaflets, and British parachutists arrived. I remember playing in the garden of Raffles Hotel where we were lodged while families were reunited and messages sent to relatives in the UK. We were very fortunate – my father had spent many months suffering deprivation and disease while working on the Siamese/Burmese Death Railway, but he was alive and came back to us. So many husbands and fathers did not return.

Soon we were on the *Monowai*, the first ship to leave for 'home'. I remember staring in wonder at the sheets, smooth, clean and white on the bunks. On arriving at Port Said we were taken to a huge hangar where long tables were heaped with clothes and all the things we needed for a hard British winter. Everything was courtesy of the Red Cross.

We arrived in Liverpool on 11 October 1945 and caught the train to Edinburgh to meet my grandmother and Aunt Rena. There, the delights of Scottish food, a house and garden, shops, Christmas and snowballs awaited me.

THE HORROR
OF BELSEN

---

17 April 1945

The following letter was written by a Mr Ashton, a British Army Liaison Officer (LO) sent into Belsen to talk to the German commander-in-charge of the camp before it was taken over by the Allied authorities.

THIS IS GOING TO BE a horrid letter. I am almost unconscious with fatigue and impotent rage.

I was sent on yesterday as an LO immediately behind the leading tanks to make contact with the commander of a concentration camp. I bagged a German prisoner, stuck him on my jeep and made him take me to the man. I was ushered into a room full of heel-clicking colonels who were expecting me. I ignored the Hitler salute and told them when we were coming and that they would meet the CO at a certain place. I think they expected us to come to them.

And now I cannot describe the rest. It is beyond the powers of description. In one camp there are 15,000 starving Europeans. In another there are 45,000. When we arrived, the SS were shooting. There were 3,000 dead bodies in a truck and another 500 in a naked heap. They were dying of starvation. Some lay on the ground moaning with holes in their stomachs. Some were trying to crawl on hands and knees – being too weak to walk – to a pile of rotten potatoes and were being potted at by the SS. We stopped all this. Oh! the pathetic sights. Emaciated skeletons weeping and moaning with joy and clinging to us.

They have become animals – starving dying animals. I saw them die of starvation at my feet. A skeleton girl clung to the CO and said, 'You are Mr Dick Taylor.' She was once his parlour maid! Typhus and typhoid are raging. 500 died last night. There are no medical supplies. They are lice-ridden. There they lie on the ground, some eating dirty swedes, some quietly dying. All crying to God and blessing us and our King. All night we remained with them and kept them calm as best we could. But they broke in – madly – and rifled what little food there was in the camp.

There has been no water and food all day. Tonight it is arriving and we are trying to feed 60,000 starving people and control them. The medical side is being tackled. But thousands more will die. It is a numbing experience but I wouldn't have avoided it. I am going down there again tonight to try to help. It is a lovely thing to be able to do – but oh! how impotent we are to do 1/100th enough.

The SS have been rounded up and taken away for trial and hanging. All of what I have said is about half as bad as it really is. It is an extermination camp. There is *no* water. It is about me being soft. I have never wanted to hate before. There is some pleasure in smashing Hitler's portraits but there is little one can do just now but be as kind as possible and shed tears of impotent rage and swear to God that this shall never happen again as far as one's power goes and that the guilty shall be punished. Even my clothes smell of death.

A QA Remembers

Brenda McBryde

Brenda McBryde is the author of A Nurse's War *(1979) and* Quiet Heroines
*(1985), the latter recalling the part played by nurses in World War II. She is also
well known for her historical novels.*

FROM ONE'S EARLIEST AWARENESS the symbol of the red cross has stood
indisputably for a Good Thing just as, in my case, Gregory's Stomach
Powder once a month was a decidedly Bad Thing. Even to a child, the
Red Cross Society meant a benevolent presence.

Now, looking back, I realise that it has always hovered within my sights, if
not within my grasp – taken for granted as a component of living, just as much
as marmalade for breakfast, but I made no actual contact until I became a
student nurse in World War II. On the wards of a northern hospital I met my
first ambassadors of the BRCS – the VADs. They wore aprons and caps, but
there any resemblance to probationer nurses ended. These young women still
had about them the heady air of independence that we students once had. Such
nonsense was quickly knocked out of a student nurse's head in those days. We
lived in a Nurses' Home, a whole world away from the commonplace of life
outside, but the VAD went home every night, away from disinfectant,
autocratic ward sisters and never-ending rules.

VADs brought a breath of fresh air to the wards. They even laughed out loud
sometimes, chatted up the patients and cuddled children. Their willingness to
help at every level gained our respect, especially since they were frequently
given the tasks that no one else wanted. We probationers were astonished that
these girls had actually volunteered to be dogsbodies. The day came, however,
when their experience on the wards and the skills they had learned were

recognised. When casualties arrived in their hundreds from Dunkirk, Alamein, Cassino and Arromanches, the hospitals would have been hard put to manage without the VADs.

Later, as a nursing sister in Queen Alexandra's Imperial Military Nursing Service, amidst all the trauma of battle in Normandy, that Red Cross symbol was constantly before my eyes in the provision of comforts for the wounded. Sharing our mess was the Red Cross Welfare Officer, who dealt sympathetically with the personal problems of the wounded and assisted the matron in the unenviable task of writing sad letters to relatives.

In Germany I remember the doubt in the eyes of men released from concentration camps when, in place of their filthy camp uniforms, we gave them Red Cross pyjamas and slippers. They felt the good stuff with disbelief. Was this another trick by Nazi guards that would end in the gas chamber? The mark of the Red Cross gave reassurance. Whatever their native language, all knew the meaning of the Red Cross.

And when I was sick to the heart with hatred for the race that could inflict such atrocities on their fellow men, I was confronted with the compassion of the German Red Cross nurses. They were young women volunteering for this work of rehabilitation. They came from Hamburg with their matron in an old van powered by a bag of consumer gas strapped to the top. I was prepared to give Rosa a hard time when she was sent to help me, but she wept when she saw the skeletal creatures, the pot bellies, the hollow-eyed skulls and shaven heads – walking medical disasters all of them. 'We did not know,' she wept. 'As God is my witness, we did not know.'

Those nurses of the German Red Cross worked all hours of the day without complaint for small thanks. The patients looked upon them with hate in their eyes. The German girls did not expect thanks, but despite my reservations, I was moved by their determination to make amends for the evil practised on these poor creatures.

Many years later, when my family was grown up, I came to know the BRCS at grass roots level in village life. It is the listening ear when depressed young mothers need help, a pair of hands to make breakfast for the bedridden, or to take a turn at driving the disabled.

I am proud to wear my Red Cross badge alongside that of the Queen Alexandra's Imperial Military Nursing Service/Reserve.

A LITTLE WOODEN HORSE

Viscountess Falmouth

The following extract comes from the 1945 diary of Viscountess Falmouth, who at the time was President of the Red Cross in Cornwall. She was accompanying the Countess of Limerick, Deputy Chairman of the Executive Committee of the War Organisation, on a visit to the British Military Hospital in Klagenfurt in the British Zone of Austria. The object of the visit was to inspect the British Red Cross team working there.

December 1st – British Military Hospital, Klagenfurt

Yesterday I had a very nice present from our Red Cross delegate. He sent me a tiny wooden carving of a horse – most beautifully done – carved from the butt of a rifle. It was presented to him by one of the Hungarians he has been befriending. Bit by bit I've pieced together the story.

It all began two or three years ago, when thousands of Hungarian peasants – some ten or twenty thousand of them – gave up their farms before the advancing Russians and trekked west with their wives and children and household goods piled on their narrow wooden carts, drawn by their stocky little short-nosed ponies. At some time they must have joined the German Army, for when the surrender came, they were all in Austria, in German uniforms and with German rifles, but, mysteriously, still with their families and carts.

In common with most Austrian prisoners they were demobilised, classed as Surrendered Personnel, and attempts were made to get them into camps. At this stage our Red Cross worker John Trevor came into the picture. This ex-Rough-Rider Sergeant of Dragoons, as a horse-lover, instantly took to the Hungarians with their ponies, and they equally took to him. He found them wandering the roads like nomads, living in fir-branch huts in the forests; he gradually part-cajoled, part-bullied them into proper huts and camps. It was no one's special business to get this particular group of tiresome ex-enemy DPs [Displaced Persons] home, but Trevor began agitating here, there and everywhere, and finally the powers-that-be sought permission from the Russians to allow them, their carts and their precious ponies through the Russian zone. As might have been expected, the Russians said, 'Certainly not!' And there the matter rested, and the unlucky Hungarians wandered up and down the roads and asked how they were to feed their little horses in winter.

Then John Trevor bestirred himself again. He put on his best coat with its fur collar, and off he went to the Russian zone. Whether or not he had British leave it's best not to enquire, but into the Russian zone he got, and he went up and down making friends with Commissars and District Commanders. No doubt he said and did a great many things which a respectable officer of the British Red Cross should not have said and done. But – he came back with a safe-conduct in his pocket, and leave for his Hungarians, their wives and children, their carts and, best of all, their little horses, to pass through the Russian zone and return in safety to their homes.

So he summoned his Hungarians to tell them the good news and that they must build camps at 15-mile points all down the roads from the French zone, the American zone, through the British, up to the Russian frontier. Fifteen camps in the US territory, and twenty-one in ours – each with huts for the women and children to sleep in, and farriers' shops and vets' standings for the horses.

Today, half are home already – ten thousand men, women and children, saved from the slow deterioration and despair of the DP camp, and – final triumph – with 7,000 of their own precious horses.

Last week we saw fifty little wagons, piled high with furnishings, led by tall, handsome women, with rosy sturdy children, and escorted by magnificent men, in the remnants of tattered field-green uniforms. They were rumbling slowly east, up a tremendous gorge, the sun catching the gay coloured handkerchiefs of the women as the carts jingled up and down the twisting mountain roads and the foals ran beside their mothers at the axle poles. They were John Trevor's Hungarians – going home. All done by one funny little ex-Sergeant Major of Dragoons!

CONTINUING STRIFE
1949–88

REFUGEES IN PALESTINE

Ella Jorden, MBE

Before joining the Red Cross, Sister Jorden belonged to a medical mission in China. Her previous Red Cross assignments had taken her to Germany, Malaya and Korea. She died in 1993, shortly after agreeing to allow this excerpt from her book, Operation Mercy, *to be published.*

HAVING SPENT THREE YEARS in a Japanese prison camp, I thought I knew the depths of misery to which humanity can sink. But I was wrong, for I had no conception of the terrible suffering that I was to find in the coming months.

Early in February 1949, accompanied by a hygiene inspector, I flew out to Damascus *en route* for Jordan and the camp which was my ultimate destination.

At the end of the British mandate in Palestine, over 300,000 Arab refugees crossed the border into Syria, Lebanon and Jordan. A British Red Cross Commission had been set up and I was to take charge of the medical work in a camp for refugees in the Jordan Valley. Driving through the valley was a beautiful sight, the grandeur of the scenery breathtaking. On our left were the mountains of Moab and the Dead Sea, ahead the dim outline of the city of Jericho, and beyond – the church towers of Jerusalem.

The camp turned out to be a huge sack-cloth settlement situated in the desert far from anywhere. Here 17,000 people were crammed together in ragged tents. As we approached, crowds of people swarmed towards us and it seemed that the whole population had gathered to watch my arrival.

Two Danish Red Cross Sisters and two British Red Cross Welfare Officers were already in the camp to welcome me. They showed me the two tents in which they lived and where to put up my camp-bed. The two tents were pitched near the water point, which was the centre of all comings and goings. Because we were a great source of curiosity, a stream of people came to stare and to find out how we lived in our tents. Our slightest movements were observed, and even when darkness fell, the flap of our tent would be lifted to enable them to take yet another peep. One family next door had a camel which bedded down just at our front door, and its puffing and snoring during the night made us feel that we really were in the desert.

Next day I was taken to the medical centre and was appalled at what I saw. The old tent which housed the centre was torn and dirty. It was where dressings were done and medicines dispensed, but it lacked even the simplest and most fundamental requirements. Everything was in short supply, which was partly because the Commission had reckoned on only a few hundred refugees, and the population of the camp had grown into thousands.

One of the first things I did was to get hold of a pile of sacks and set an Arab tailor to stitch them together. This made a sort of curtain and gave some privacy for the doctor's tent – for his thrice-weekly visit from the hospital 30 miles away were always red-letter days.

According to reports, there were hundreds of deaths a week, but no one could say with any certainty what the death rate was, since deaths were always kept secret because a reduction in the numbers of a family meant a reduction in their food rations. The monthly ration was just enough to keep people alive, and although various nations sent food from Europe, the Arab people found it difficult to accept anything new and foreign, however nourishing it was. The Swiss Government, for instance, made a valuable present of a large quantity of cheese. One group of refugees refused to eat it, not only because they preferred their local goats' milk, but because they were not going to eat cheese with holes in it!

Clothes were another difficulty, many refugees preferring to rip pieces off their ragged tents to wearing Western clothes.

In the early days two Arab schoolboys attached themselves to the Danish Sister and myself at the medical centre. They quickly learned to sterilise the instruments and to prepare the tables for dressings. With enough English to translate simple sentences for us, they were invaluable at shepherding the crowds, directing them to come in by the entrance and go out by the exit, thus reducing the customary chaos.

It was the policy to employ as many refugees as possible, and eventually more than 1,000 Palestinians were on the salaried staff. We could not have coped without their knowledge of different dialects, local customs and traditions. Knowing no Arabic, I had to speak to my patients through an interpreter. Fortunately, an intelligent young Arab, who had worked with the

British medical department in Palestine, came forward. But the fact that Hussein was a man proved a little embarrassing at times – especially when I attended midwifery cases. As the only trained European midwife among 17,000 people, I could only look after the most difficult cases, but however critical the confinement, under no circumstances could a man be allowed where a woman was in childbirth. Hussein had to remain outside and the translations took place through tent walls.

As time went by and there were still only five of us attending to the wants of so many refugees, we knew we must have more staff and more supplies before the hot weather inevitably brought the danger of epidemics. Then we had news which brought us great hope. We were to be given the opportunity of making an appeal for funds through the BBC, not only for ourselves, but for another British Red Cross camp in the Jordan Valley. It seemed a wonderful idea until, to my horror, I received a note saying that it was me who should go to London to make the appeal.

I was told that everyone making a first broadcast found the experience nerve-wracking. Frankly, I was terrified. After the rehearsal, I walked home feeling depressed. I felt that I had not put over the awful suffering and urgency of the situation with enough force to reach both the hearts of the listeners and their purses. As I walked the London streets, the words I wanted to say suddenly seemed to come to me, and on the Sunday evening I was able to describe something more than 'just another refugee camp' to my listeners.

People listened and responded magnificently. Girls and boys sent in their pennies, pensioners sent stamps, Christians and Jews joined in subscribing to help the starving and homeless Arabs. I felt particularly humbled when I read some of the letters. It was my first experience of the wonderful generosity of the British public, which, I discovered, is ever ready to answer the call for help from the uprooted and the homeless. I could not wait to get back to Jordan to tell them what we were to receive in the way of aid and supplies. I took back with me as much medical equipment as I was allowed on the plane and the promise that more Red Cross personnel were to follow.

In the following year came discussions on the future of our work and its take-over by the United Nations. It is always a heartbreak to leave the people one has been working among, but it is inevitable, as the mission of the Red Cross is to act as a bridge between emergency and the time when people can be looked after by their government or some other organisation – in this case the United Nations. On the last day of April 1950 the Red Cross flags, which for 16 months had flown over the two camps in Jordan, were lowered. Our work was done.

THE WINDS OF CHANGE

Brian Hodgson, CMG

Mr. Hodgson was Director General of the British Red Cross Society, 1970–74. For his important contribution to the work of the International movement he was awarded the Henry Dunant medal in 1993.

AFTER THE WAR AND THROUGHOUT the 1950s and 1960s the British Red Cross Society was called upon to respond to new challenges in the countries where it had established Overseas Branches. The progressive erosion of colonial ties in the run-up to independence in many territories sometimes gave rise to political tensions and dangers, with partial breakdown of law and order, in which the local people required special help. Often the local Red Cross Branches were unable to give this help owing to political sensitivities.

The Society's answer was to recruit Overseas Field Officers, trained in nursing and welfare, who were not involved in local politics. In the early years their duties were more of an emergency nature – as in Malaya and Kenya – but many of them stayed on during the 1960s, and after independence were able to use their experience to help with the orderly transition from Branch status to that of an independent National Red Cross Society.

To pay full tribute to the achievements of these British Red Cross ambassadors would justify a Roll of Honour. Suffice it to say that their efforts assisted no fewer than 24 existing National Societies to achieve international recognition as full members of the Movement. The following are two examples of the type of 'emergency duties' which these officers undertook:

Malaya, 1952–57

The emergency in Malaya arose from the widespread activities of communist-led guerrillas, who used terror as an effective weapon. Government policy was to concentrate the rural population into 'new villages' which could more easily be defended. Medical and health facilities, however, were entirely lacking and far beyond the scope of local resources. The British Red Cross was asked to help, and within a short period had recruited and equipped 25 medical/welfare teams, each with its own Land Rover.

The teams lived in temporary huts and moved around by day, but at night were restricted by curfew, like their charges, behind barbed wire. Each team was responsible for some 15 villages, with populations varying from 500–4,000, and clinics and dispensaries were set up in each village.

When travelling between their villages, the teams had no protection other than the Red Cross, despite the fact that the guerrillas made a speciality of ambushing vehicles. The remarkable fact must be recorded, however, that a letter was delivered to the teams' HQ from the leader of the guerrillas undertaking not to attack any Red Cross vehicle. He merely requested that a large Red Cross be painted on the roof of each Land Rover so that it could more easily be seen by snipers in the jungle tree-tops. In four years of constant local warfare, no Red Cross team was ever attacked or ambushed.

Although their work was confined to health clinics and welfare activities, the very presence of the teams conferred a measure of 'protection' in the best and widest sense as intended by the Geneva Conventions. The respect in which they were held by the villagers – Chinese, Malayan, Indian and Javanese – was demonstrated by the practical support the teams received throughout the emergency period. This did much to lay the foundations for the successful Malaysian Red Crescent Society of today.

Zanzibar Revolt, 1963

Janet Adams and Ella Jorden, two of the most experienced nursing Field Officers, were sent to Zanzibar late in 1963 to help establish a National Society, and were in the town when the revolutionary coup took place immediately following the Sultan's hurried departure. It was led by an African named Okello, who ruled briefly, but brutally, before being superseded by Abdi Karume.

Several hundred Arabs and Asians were killed outright as Zanzibar succumbed to mob rule, and over 5,000 were rounded up and imprisoned in the large Aga Khan School, where they were detained for days with little food or water. Janet and Ella were among the few Europeans to venture out from their homes and witness some of the atrocities. Janet also managed to visit the school and was horrified at what she found there as many of the overcrowded inhabitants were also wounded. The two nurses promptly started work with what equipment they could find, but for Janet the final straw was the wanton destruction by Okello's 'soldiers' of her Red Cross glass feeding bottles for the babies; this was on the grounds that the bottles could be used as weapons.

Outraged by all this and relying only on her righteous indignation and her Red Cross uniform, she stormed into Okello's HQ in the Sultan's palace, brushing aside armed guards, and demanded bandages for the wounded and help in feeding and watering the captives. Okello was so surprised by this apparition that he agreed to her demands and said she could use the Medical Department stores and recruit local staff to help. To their eternal credit, several of the local medical staff agreed to work with her. The great need was for blood for the wounded. The few local Europeans gave what they could that night, but much more was needed, so the following day Janet was personally rowed out to the British naval ship which was in the harbour and got her quota of blood from the crew.

As things quietened down, conditions improved and eventually it was arranged to evacuate most of the Arabs and Asians. Undoubtedly, Janet Adams' single-handed intervention saved many lives and alleviated suffering on a large scale. A closer resemblance to the actions of Henry Dunant at Solferino would indeed be hard to find.

The East Coast Floods

Ann Hopkin

Formerly a Red Cross Service Hospitals' Welfare Officer, with wide experience of overseas work, Ann Hopkin had just taken up a post at National Headquarters when terrible floods struck eastern England in 1953.

O<small>N THE NIGHT OF</small> 31 J<small>ANUARY</small> 1953 the worst floods in living memory devastated the coastlines of Lincolnshire, Norfolk, Suffolk, Essex and the southeast corner of Kent.

At 8 a.m. on Sunday, 1 February the Red Cross stores at Lewisham went into action, following an emergency call received from the Essex Branch. Throughout that day and for many more weeks, supplies were sent out to all the affected areas. Everything from mops, buckets, brooms and cleaning materials, to mattresses, pillows, linoleum and mats were forwarded for distribution from the Branch's HQ stores.

A nationwide appeal was swiftly launched for clothing, bedding and household effects, and within a few days two central Red Cross depots were opened and were receiving a steady flow of goods in Cambridge and Nottingham. Red Cross members, university students and hundreds of other volunteers unpacked, checked and repackaged goods for dispatch to the coast. Up and down the country other Red Cross Branches made their own collections and offered volunteers to relieve personnel in the affected areas.

Daily conferences were held at our National Headquarters in London, and the Society, together with the WVS and St John, were invited to join the Home

Office Emergency Committee which met every day. The GPO installed additional telephone lines to my office as our switchboard was already overloaded. People called to offer temporary shelter, to foster children, and, of course, to enquire anxiously about families and relatives.

Yes, National Headquarters was indeed busy, but it was in the county Branches that the full horror of the floods was felt, and it was there that many acts of bravery and resourcefulness took place. County by county we learned of the help given by Red Cross members.

Lincolnshire

At midnight on Saturday, 31 January, the police alerted the local Detachment at Mabelthorpe. The County Director and Welfare Officer were called and a police van was put at their disposal. This was loaded with blankets, which were delivered to a rest centre by 3 a.m. when the first 'refugees' were brought in. Supplies continued to arrive, the vans being immediately unloaded and sent off to collect more refugees. Eventually some 8,000 people were brought to safety.

First-aid posts and canteens were manned continually for the hundreds of servicemen and civilians engaged on repairing the beaches, with members coming to help from places as far away as Cheshire, Glamorgan and Hampshire. Nurseries were established so mothers were free to tackle the job of cleaning up their homes, and stocks of household items were collected for later distribution to people returning to their homes.

Norfolk

The villages of Blakeney, Cley, Salthouse and Wiveton suffered most severely. First news of the floods was telephoned from the district nurse at Cley, who was herself a Red Cross member. Cley Street was like a river, drains had burst, electricity failed and furniture floated everywhere.

The rescue work was extremely hazardous, and there were many stories of heroism. One member rescued an old couple from their upstairs room by swimming in through the window. (She was later honoured by the Queen.) Another, arriving at Salthouse, found houses demolished and one woman drowned. She managed to get an elderly couple out through their upstairs window, only to become a casualty herself when she fell over a drowned cow.

Suffolk

Red Cross members were instantly active in Lowestoft, Southwold and

Ipswich. The Branch headquarters had enough stocks of bedding for the first night, which were rapidly replaced from our stores in London.

Daily cleaning parties of up to 120 members worked in Felixstowe. County officers navigated their way between fallen trees and flotsam blown in from the sea to visit every flooded village with immediate supplies. They were told about the occupants of one cottage in a remote village who refused to move. Having finally found the cottage, they were greeted by an elderly man who looked at their uniforms and called to his wife, 'It's all right, it's the Red Cross.' Obviously they were much relieved that the visitors were not going to make them leave their home.

Essex

The Red Cross began its relief effort at 3 a.m. on Sunday, 1 February, and during the initial 24 hours up to 250 members were constantly at full stretch in the Benfleet–Canvey Island area.

At Thurrock four rest centres were established, housing 1,200 refugees, while Orsett Hospital and adjacent transit camps were supported by Essex members supplemented by volunteers from London and Middlesex Branches.

The hotels in Clacton gave shelter to refugees, and the Red Cross visited them daily to ensure their needs were met. A control centre coordinated the effort from Clacton Divisional Headquarters, and a diagnosis clinic was set up in the town.

Much time was also given by members in assisting the exhausted frogmen and other civilian workers engaged in helping the rescue work along the entire coast.

As the second relief phase began, the Red Cross helped move the more fortunate back to their homes, while continuing to support the people still housed in rest camps, caravans and other billets. The Branch carried on working with flood victims well into 1954.

Kent

A representative of Erith Borough Council called at the Red Cross Commandant's house asking for help. Belvedere Marshes had flooded during Saturday night and about 500 people, mostly gypsies, had lost all their possessions.

The members of the local Detachment were having their weekly meeting when they were asked to arrange temporary accommodation in a nearby hall. Half-soaked and half-clothed men, women, children and babies were brought in by the police, having been rescued by boat. Emergency amenities were organised by the local council, and school wash-places were opened up by the borough sanitary engineer.

All medical arrangements were the responsibility of the Red Cross under the Ministry of Health. Sickness ranged from pneumonia, appendicitis, and cuts and bruises to one case of childbirth in the emergency tent. The Red Cross supplied all the necessary equipment and baby linen, and two members were asked to name the baby and become its godparents.

We are fortunate in Britain that natural disasters of the magnitude of the 1953 floods so rarely occur. For all those who suffered during that frightening winter, however, and for those in the Red Cross engaged in the relief work, the images of the east coast floods will long remain. They hold vivid memories of what can happen when the mighty sea takes over, and the ever-present danger that exists for those who live around the coastline of these British Isles.

YOUNG CORONATION VISITORS

Lois Dowler

Miss Dowler held several senior posts at National Headquarters including Director, Junior Red Cross, 1966–73

THE YOUTH SECTION OF THE British Red Cross is not, of course, as old as its parent body – a mere 71 in 1995. Nevertheless, it is interesting to recall that no less a person than Henry Dunant himself called upon children to help him as water carriers in the awful aftermath of Solferino, recognising that often the best and most enthusiastic help comes from the youngest of people.

Within the British Red Cross there are several conflicting documents as to when the Junior Red Cross Section received official recognition. In spite of records going back to 1921, our Junior Section was officially formed in 1924, and Wales has the distinction of having raised the first group.

Perhaps one of the greatest highlights of our Youth Section was in 1953 when the Executive Committee of the British Red Cross invited two Junior Red Cross members from each of the Red Cross Societies of the Commonwealth – Australia, Canada, India, New Zealand, Pakistan and South Africa – and 21 from British Red Cross Branches overseas, to see the Coronation of our present Queen. By accepting this invitation they would 'join us in our demonstration of affection and loyalty for our President, The Queen'. Thus it was on 25 May 1953 that 33 young people, with an average age of about 15, gathered at our National Training Centre in Surrey, together with 16 young representatives from all over the United Kingdom.

Although the focal point of the trip was to be the Coronation itself, there were many other highlights. The Red Cross county Branches were truly magnificent in their entertainment of the young guests and in helping to defray the cost of the visit. Altogether three Scottish, four Welsh and 30 English Branches entertained one or other of the visitors for several days in a most imaginative way. They, in turn, were rewarded by meeting some remarkable young people who, from the oldest aged 19 (from Kenya) to the youngest aged 11 (from Sierra Leone), were excellent ambassadors of their countries and their National Societies.

A visit to the National Training Centre by the Commandant-in-Chief, The Princess Royal, gave each delegate an opportunity to put on an exhibition in the garden depicting some aspects of each country represented and their Red Cross activities. Not a drop of rain fell on us all day long which, in the light of what happened two days later, was nothing short of a miracle.

On 2 June we rose at 4.15 a.m. after a cold, uncomfortable night 'camping' at our National Headquarters in London, and set off on foot for our appointed places. Our overseas guests had seats allocated in Parliament Square, while the UK delegates were seated in Piccadilly by Green Park. Surely nobody needs reminding about how wet the weather was that day nor even, several soaking hours later, how wonderful the procession was – 'a sea of colour', one young guest wrote – 'uniforms, regalia, medals, swords, white hats, red coats, black bearskins' which took nearly an hour to pass us. It seems hardly possible, with the cheering of the crowds, the massed bands and the pipers, that sleep could overcome you, but if you are only 11, have come all the way from Sierra Leone and have been up since 4 a.m., perhaps it does. Anyway, 'They woke me when the Gold Coach came,' said Alice.

Eventually, having been in our seats since 6 a.m., we all returned by coach to the Training Centre at Barnett Hill that evening and saw the Coronation all over again on the relatively new wonder of a black and white television set.

That historic occasion was why we had all come together, but every bit as important was how much we learned from each other in those days at Barnett Hill. This was our opportunity in the British Red Cross of showing our gratitude to the people of the Commonwealth for all their help during the war, but it was also our good fortune to have the privilege of bringing together young people from all corners of the world.

From the very beginning we lived together in the greatest possible harmony and happiness, and one of my own best memories is the sight of young people from some 28 countries crowded round the piano, all singing Scottish, Irish and Welsh songs in perfect English!

THE HUNGARIAN
UPRISING, 1956

Nanette Bryce, MBE, JP

Nanette Bryce joined the Red Cross as a VAD during World War II. She has worked with the Cheshire Branch ever since. Her particular contribution to the Society has been as Voluntary Administrator for the northern Pontin Red Cross Holiday Camps that have taken place annually since 1970.

Early in December 1956, as just one of over 30 people attending a hastily called selection committee at Red Cross National Headquarters in London set up as a result of the Hungarian Uprising in Budapest, I began to speculate why anybody, including myself, should volunteer for such an operation. We were a mixed bag from which a team of eight would be chosen to run the second British Red Cross Hungarian Refugee Camp in Austria. Having been interviewed – it actually seemed more like an interrogation – it did not take too long to learn the result. In my case, I was told to get kitted out and have the necessary jabs for the assignment in Hungary.

Six days later, wakening in an icy cold room, I found myself in Schloss Liechtenstein, which turned out to be about 20 miles from Vienna. This was a 'family camp' where groups were never separated, and it accommodated approximately 500 adults and children in large dormitories with very little privacy.

At the beginning conditions were appalling, with no sanitation other than hastily dug latrines in the courtyard, some cold running water and inadequate washing facilities. So ill-equipped were the kitchens that hot meals had to be delivered from a local hospital.

On arrival, the refugees were mostly in a state of shock and their main requirements were a sense of security, warmth and food in that order. The last commodity was a problem for everybody. To begin with, there was not very much of it, and at that time of year very little fresh vegetables or fruit. Serving the meals also posed problems, but we soon introduced meal tickets (with special ones for babies and children under 14) which put a stop to many of the refugees coming back again and again for more food.

Living arrangements were equally bad for the Red Cross personnel. Our toilet facilities were nil, so we came to an arrangement with the caretaker of the Schloss to use the toilet in his flat. This had its funny side. First it was agreed there would only be two visits per day – once at 8 a.m. and once at 8 p.m. – because the family went to bed at 8.30. These visits were further complicated by the presence of a fierce Dobermann, which had been acquired during the Russian occupation to protect the virtue of the caretaker's daughters. The dog had to be locked up in the larder at prescribed 'loo times'. This being achieved, we sat in the kitchen awaiting our respective turns. On New Year's Eve, during our evening visit, we drank a toast in cognac supplied by the caretaker as we waited to fulfil the calls of nature.

Clothing was another major problem which had to be solved during the first few weeks of camp organisation. Initially we discovered that much of the clothing from our stores was finding its way into local pawn shops in the town. Another difficulty was that some people, it seemed, had off-loaded their unwanted and, in some cases, unwashed, garments on us. We unpacked out-of-season summer clothes, bags of left-footed shoes and what appeared to be pre-1914 dresses. The unwanted clothes were sent off to scrap merchants and with the money raised, winter clothes were bought for the refugees in our camp. Gradually, things improved, and by early March we were able to supply sewing machines, irons, shoe-making tools and good clothing. Workshops were set up to employ people and a kindergarten was started to help the young mothers.

Tragedy and hardship often seem harder to bear when they occur during holidays such as Christmas. But the refugees in our camp were determined to make the best of things during the festive season. For days before Christmas we were inundated with requests for electric light bulbs – surely they could not be failing at *that* rate! At the same time there was the mysterious disappearance of wooden beds and electrical wiring. On Christmas Eve we knew the answer. At the back of the Schloss was a high rock formation, and as darkness fell an enormous illuminated cross appeared. It was so bright that we were informed it was interfering with aircraft landings at Vienna airport, so much to everyone's regret it had to be switched off.

It was a memorable Christmas all the same. Nearly everything that came out of the kitchen was a triumph of ingenuity, and our Christmas Eve dinner of fried fish and fried potatoes was no exception. Each child received a parcel and every family had a spruce bough and candles; why the Schloss didn't go up in flames I shall never know. For this Red Cross volunteer it was an image I shall never forget.

I had many interesting experiences during my time helping the Hungarian refugees, not only on two tours of duty in two separate camps, but also as a Red Cross escort on the trains that crossed Europe to England. There the refugees were dispersed to camps while awaiting emigration to the USA and Canada. On the long Continental journey we were supported by each Red Cross Society of the country through which we passed. Sometimes the experiences were harrowing, often they were fatiguing, but frequently they were humorous. At no time during the aftermath of the Hungarian Uprising did I regret my decision to volunteer for this particular job in my Red Cross life.

THE ABERFAN DISASTER

Viscount Tonypandy, PC, DCL

THE MORNING OF 19 OCTOBER 1966 was pleasantly autumnal as I left my house in Cardiff for the Welsh Office, Cathays Park, where I was serving as Minister of State. It was 9.45 a.m. when I received an urgent message from Selwyn Jones, Town Clerk at Merthyr Tydfil. In a voice throbbing with emotion he told me: 'We have sustained a disaster at Aberfan. It is a major disaster, for a coal tip on the mountainside has slid down and enveloped the infant and junior school, where we believe that there are over 120 children.'

Having alerted all the major emergency authorities, both voluntary and statutory, I left Cardiff for Aberfan. Although I did not realise it at the time, my life was to be linked with Aberfan for the rest of my days. By the time I arrived at the scene of the disaster, local men were frantically digging to reach the teachers and the children beneath the tip rubble. I was told that after the first ten minutes no one had been brought out alive. I stepped over the bodies that had been reached by the experienced miners, who were themselves related to the tragic victims.

It would have been easy to panic in the presence of such overwhelming grief, but instead there was just an intense concentration on the two overriding tasks – rescue work and comforting of the bereaved. It was only in retrospect that I realised how I had taken for granted the presence of the Red Cross, the Salvation Army and other voluntary workers.

A local Nonconformist chapel had been accepted for use as our temporary mortuary. As the bodies were lifted from the rubble, they were gently laid side by side. Ambulances conveyed them to Bethania Chapel where, under the superb leadership of Miss Miriam Jowett, Red Cross workers joined with the Salvation Army and others in washing the little bodies and laying them on the chapel seats until the parents could come to identify them.

As if by a miracle, a few young teachers, who had been in a less-affected part of the school, had survived the disaster. They bravely looked at each little body after it had been washed and attached a name tag so that the grieving parents could be taken straight to their loved one's body for identification.

The quiet strength of the Red Cross workers, who had been trained to practise self-control in a crisis, was a blessing for us all. During the whole period a rota of 30 members served on duty in three eight-hour shifts throughout day and night. Although the main burden of work naturally fell to the Glamorganshire Branch, support was also forthcoming from other Red Cross Branches. Worcestershire, Monmouthshire, Carmarthenshire, Gloucestershire, Warwickshire, Bristol, Herefordshire and Buckinghamshire all gave vital and invaluable assistance.

Red Cross assistance was by no means limited to washing the children's bodies and to comforting the bereaved families. A first aid post was established on the disaster site so that help was available for any of the army of voluntary workers who were themselves injured in the course of their dangerous rescue work. Tea and food was provided to sustain them in the grisly task. Meanwhile, a Red Cross Enquiry Centre was set up in a dry cleaner's shop opposite Bethania Chapel. Would-be helpers flocked there to offer their help.

As the school registers had been lost in the rubble, it was necessary to assemble the parents to discover which children had been at school when the disaster occurred. This was the most harrowing experience of my entire public life. Parents and relatives frantic with grief came to give the names of their little ones who were missing. I shared their sorrow and was grateful beyond measure for the steadfastness of the Red Cross.

A second Red Cross Enquiry Centre was set up outside the cinema and acted as a rest centre for exhausted workers. More Red Cross helpers laboured through night and day to keep it running efficiently. Blankets, bedding and other equipment were distributed from the Red Cross store, and it seemed to me, as I visited every home which had suffered bereavement, that there was a Red Cross presence in every street in Aberfan. Indeed, Miriam Jowett, the Director, told me that over 700 Red Cross workers laboured continuously in the stricken village.

We are fortunate in the United Kingdom to know that we have such a formidable force of trained and resourceful personnel who constitute the British Red Cross. It is inspiring that whatever emergency occurs, the Red Cross Movement is ready to provide skilled and dedicated help.

HURRICANE JANET

Janet Adams, MBE

Mention has already been made of the service given by Janet Adams in Zanzibar. Her outstanding work as a Red Cross delegate around the world was recognised by the ICRC with its highest award for nurses, the Florence Nightingale Medal.

In THE EARLY AUTUMN, Atlantic hurricanes occur with monotonous regularity, frequently blowing themselves harmlessly into oblivion. In 1955 nine such minor storms petered out. But on 24 September the next one, codenamed 'Janet', hit the Windward Isles with devastating force, leaving a trail of destruction that stretched from Grenada, Carriacou and Barbados to Mexico.

The following day the Governor of the Windward Islands flew over the disaster area in a US naval seaplane, assessed the damage and appealed for aid. He reported that Carriacou, a small island 30 miles north of Grenada, had caught the full force of the hurricane and only two buildings were left standing. In Grenada the devastation by wind and sea had flattened everything. Rivers had run amok, bridges were broken or swept away and there were landslides everywhere. The airport was deep in mud and littered with wrenched-up trees. Gouyave, a small town on the leeward coast, looked as though it had suffered an aerial bombardment. The whole island wore a coat of brown. In St George, the capital, the powerhouse was flooded, the reservoir silted up and the prison and mental home damaged. Nowhere on the island had light, water, power or telephones. The roads had also disappeared.

The immediate problems on both islands were food, water, communications and relief for the homeless. Reports of fatalities began to be received: 115 in Grenada and 25 in Carriacou. There were also many injured, with fractures and deep gashes from galvanised roofs hurtling around. As communications improved, it was feared that more casualties might be reported.

In Grenada, emergency powers came into force. A Central Relief Committee was immediately established, with sub-committees in parishes and districts. Power and water were restored within two days, an amazing achievement by the technicians, who worked flat out around the clock, despite the fact that most of them had acute worries about their own families and homes.

When the Governor's assessment of needs was announced, the neighbouring islands started loading relief supplies, even though some of them had also suffered from the hurricane. The first relief ship bound for Grenada sailed from Trinidad on 24 September carrying 7,000 lb of clothing, 25 tons of food, 22 crates of medical supplies, 900 sheets of galvanised iron and 25 kegs of nails. All were gifts from the government, the Red Cross, St John and individual donors. This shipment was closely followed by a US destroyer carrying American Red Cross tents, blankets and cots.

Soon a flotilla of schooners and yachts were delivering gifts from other small neighbouring islands. Airlines and shipping companies offered free freight, and within a week the harbour had filled up with assorted cargoes. Everything had to be loaded on to lighters (barges lent by Trinidad) and transported to stores or delivered round the island. Virtually everyone helped in some way or another. For several weeks the only shelter at night were the stone churches, which people crowded into. Slowly but surely the people began to climb out of the calamity, cheered by the immense concern and generosity of the caring world.

At home in Scotland, amusing myself happily on the banks of the River Spey, a telephone call from Red Cross HQ promptly dispatched me with a tent to Grenada, followed a day or two later by Jana Clapham, Director of the Bahamian Branch of the BRCS, who was destined to live in my tent in Carriacou. I, however, joined Kelvin Diaz and Beatrice Oliveria (volunteers from the Trinidad Branch of BRCS) in the delightful but somewhat overcrowded hotel in Grenada; it had four engineers to a room and a rather leaky roof, but I was lucky and got a room to myself.

Kelvin, a tall, elegant schoolteacher, worked with the Central Relief Committee, and Beatrice, who was older and also a teacher, worked in the Red Cross store. I myself was assigned to work with the Emergency Committee set up in each parish and district. I devoted my time exclusively to getting the needs of the inhabitants screened and recorded and issuing food tickets to every needy person. Each night I returned to hand my lists to the Emergency Committee.

In the Red Cross stores the volunteers had a colossal job. Theirs was the task of sending the goods out around the island as guided by the lists from the

Emergency Committee. Food, clothing, pots and pans, blankets and goodness knows what else were dispatched daily. Regrettably, on occasions, some goods, such as galvanised roofing and wood, were spirited away from ship to shore and shore to oblivion. Kelvin sometimes rode 'shot gun' on top of the lorry to see that nothing slipped off *en route* by mistake.

I seldom set foot inside the store, but I do remember one consignment in particular – a glittering pile of satin evening sandals in peacock colours with diamond and sequin-studded heels. Sadly, the islanders pounding about in the mud of their ruined homes had no use for such pretty things, but I liked to think that later, in happier days, dainty feet would enjoy twirling round the dance floor, grateful for the gift from the Aruba ladies.

My job was not nearly as hard as that of the stores staff, but it was sadder as each day I saw those who had lost so much. As I travelled round in my battered taxi, I was appalled by the devastation. Houses were, as the Grenadians would say, 'all mashed up', meaning as flat as pancakes. Rescued clothing and bedding were draped around to dry out and a few bedraggled chickens scavenged about gloomily. Everywhere people were coping stoically with the disaster and I was lost in admiration for their pluck, charm and good nature.

One day, most unexpectedly, a Land Rover turned up – a gift from Trinidad. Thereafter, floods and non-existent roads presented no problem and I was able to squash passengers in on top of the supplies I carried. Travelling up and down each day I began to recognise people, and each day I ate my lunch on a rock beside the road. If it was raining, I would call on the Catholic priest and eat my snack in his house. Once, when I arrived dripping wet, he insisted that I have a tot of 'mountain dew', the locally brewed rum. To his great amusement, as I drank the tot, I had to clutch the top of my head because it felt as though it was lifting off. I vowed then to steer clear of such delights in the future.

Early in December, Kelvin and I decided to join the first passenger-carrying sloop sailing for the island of Carriacou. We wanted to see how our two fellow Red Cross colleagues were faring. The destruction on Carriacou was pitiful. Nevertheless, the people of this small fishing and farming community pulled together to restore their lives, helped by the relief supplies and their own stalwart characters. It was good to see our friends again and to learn what a spectacularly good job they were doing. Jana had borrowed a bicycle on which she rode everywhere, cooking for the relief team on a battered stove and washing up in the sea. The Polish doctor, whose hospital and home had been demolished, was heroic. He and his staff worked night and day, and his wife and small daughters were homeless until the tents arrived.

Before I ended my assignment on Grenada, I held a 'maroon' in a distant village to the north of the island. In the West Indies a 'maroon' is a community effort to erect a new building. The women cook and the men and boys build the house. In this case, I had asked the local committee to agree to build a house for two old ladies whose home had been 'all mashed up'. They agreed at once. The relief store provided a barrel of salted pigs' feet – a present, I think, from Newfoundland or Canada – flour for dumplings, beans and also the building materials and some furniture. I bought some white rum from the rum factory.

The men set to, helped and hindered by excited children, dancing round, dragging branches, giggling, chattering and generally enjoying themselves. The women started a fire and began to cook. By 4 o'clock the house was nearly finished, so I left the scene, gathering up the smaller children, packing them into the Land Rover and lurching down to the beach below. The children erupted across the sand into the sea, whooping, laughing and splashing, and I joined in the fun. When we were exhausted, we piled into the Land Rover and drove back up the hill to the new house. There it stood, finished and beautiful, the frame made of tree trunks, the walls and roof of palm branches, and the door and windows made from packing cases. It was a lovely home, begun at 9 a.m. and finished by 5.30 p.m. The old ladies would live in it until a wooden house could be built, then their temporary home would be turned into a Red Cross community centre for church services, dances and meetings.

We gathered round for our feast with lots of speeches and laughter, the two old ladies each sitting on a chair with an extra one alongside for a visitor. We put the names of all 40 men who had built the house into a hat and we drew out ten lucky winners, each of whom was given a hammer or a saw. This was a great success as they had never before seen such a fair method of giving anything away.

I waved goodbye to my new friends in Grenada with true sadness. If I ever get to heaven, I will hunt around for Kelvin and Beatrice. They will certainly be there.

On Both Sides of the Bogside

Aileen McCorkell, OBE

Aileen McCorkell is President of the Western Red Cross Branch, a Trustee of the Northern Ireland Council and wife of the Lord Lieutenant for County Londonderry.

Derry or Londonderry, whichever you prefer to call it, is situated on the River Foyle in Northern Ireland, close to the border with the Republic of Ireland. On 5 October 1968 the first Civil Rights march was held in Derry. Fighting broke out between the demonstrators and the police and nearly 100 people were treated for injuries in Altnagelvin Hospital. I soon realised there must be a part for the Red Cross to play on such occasions. How could we, members of the greatest humanitarian organisation in the world, stand by and do nothing?

The situation at that time was very explosive, marches and riots occurred periodically, and then, early in 1969, barricades made of burnt-out cars, rubble and rubbish were erected by the people of the Bogside to keep the police out. There was immediate reaction to the barricades from a number of our Red Cross members. There are always people who are genuinely nervous, luckily we had a hard core of members who were prepared to carry on with Red Cross work in any adversity.

On the afternoon of 12 August 1969, reports of fighting started coming in. Each year on this day the Apprentice Boys of Derry parade to commemorate the lifting of the siege imposed on the city by King James II in 1689. Many people predicted there would be trouble, particularly as the march passed close to the Bogside, a predominantly Catholic area outside the city walls. Ferocious fighting did indeed ensue as local residents erected barricades and hurled stones and petrol bombs at the police. As evening came, numerous fires could be seen burning, flames and smoke reaching high into the sky. Red Cross members were put on standby but nobody called us out. Anxiety mounted with each news bulletin, and by the next morning I could remain inactive no longer.

I phoned up my Red Cross deputy and we agreed to go to the Bogside and see how our meals-on-wheels pensioners were surviving. There were huge barricades everywhere and now they were manned by men with clubs and sticks. We managed to get my Morris Minor through the corner of one of them and then drove into the heart of the Bogside. The fighting was going on about 100 yards away, but all around me seemed quite calm and there were lots of children playing in the streets. I was sitting in the car when I saw two boys I knew in the Order of Malta Ambulance Corps. They welcomed me with open arms: 'Come on up to the first aid post. We have a suspected appendix, a child with a fractured finger and no transport.'

At that time the Bogside was very dilapidated and the house of the suspected appendix case was indescribably awful. The agitated mother complained vociferously that the local doctor had refused to visit her sick child. We simply wrapped the five-year-old boy in a blanket and set off to Altnagelvin Hospital, picking up the 'fractured finger' at the first aid post on the way. We left the area by another route, which meant crossing another barricade, but those manning it simply waved us through when they saw the Red Cross on my car.

Later I returned by the same route and went to the Order of Malta first aid post. It was crowded with people and everyone seemed in a panic. The air was full of CS gas and our eyes began to sting. A rumour had started that it was poisonous. I did my best to dispel the rumour and calm people down. The funny part was that there were still children on the streets, even pushing their young brothers and sisters about, despite the gas in the air.

The Order of Malta first aid post was in a very small sweet shop, and when I arrived there were several casualties being treated by an enthusiastic young doctor. Meanwhile a number of the Order's first aiders were treating casualties in the fighting line. Those who needed medical attention were brought to the first aid post by ambulance. The only other vehicle that seemed to have no trouble getting through was a large red mail van, which thundered past at regular intervals.

I spent many hours in this first aid post and I was always treated exceptionally well. Naturally, some people were suspicious of me, and indeed one of my fellow Red Cross members was attacked by a man who grabbed her badge and said, 'You are the British Red Cross. Get to hell out of here.' She took no notice. To work in such situations you simply have to lose your identity, concentrate on the work and not listen to the chatter going on around you. Some people get hot under the collar when they hear things that perhaps go against their principles. I made up my mind early on to follow the principles upon which the Red Cross is based: humanity and impartiality. Had those who criticised the Derry Red Cross for going into the Bogside been there themselves, they would have seen what motivated our presence in the area – the suffering of hundreds of innocent victims who just happened to live there.

The atmosphere in the Bogside during the riots is something I shall never forget – a mixture of excitement and fear. I can only liken it to the day war broke out in 1939, when young people could not wait to join up and find adventure. Something of that spirit overcame me later when a burly man with an enormous wooden club approached me and asked if I would help evacuate three families living in a Protestant area who had received threats of being burnt out. 'You could go and I couldn't,' he added. I did go: two of the families had already gone, but the third I knew well as they were members of our Red Cross Thursday Club for handicapped people: the wife was in a wheelchair. When I told her that I had been sent to take her to the safety of her daughter's house in Creggan, she said she would think about it if I came back later! I was eventually summoned to collect her later that evening and on the way to her daughter's we drove past an open-air petrol-bomb factory. Hundreds of milk bottles were filled and waiting for the big red mail van which I had noticed earlier to transport them to the front line. Nearby was a large barricade where children were helping vigilantes to stop cars. The danger they were in, sitting beside all that petrol, still makes my blood run cold. My own car was waved through.

The next day, Thursday, 14 August, I went back to the Bogside. Most people had been up all night, so there were very few volunteers to staff the first aid post. Our meals-on-wheels team went out as usual and found several of the pensioners locked in their houses, terrified, with hardly a thing to eat. They dared not go out for fear of getting caught up in the troubles.

Casualties continued to arrive at the post, including a boy aged about twelve, who had a huge burn on his arm. After dressing it, I told him to go home and get some painkillers. His answer was, 'Give me my dustbin lid and let me get at 'em.' This was one of Ireland's young freedom fighters in 1969. I dreaded to think what paths they would follow after this taste of power, but I was not there to reason why – I had a job to do.

During the afternoon I went to see the parish priest about evacuating some children and learned that the British Army was marching into the city. To some the troops' arrival was a relief, as the fierce fighting would stop; to others it was a disappointment, the end of the most exciting three days in their young lives.

For a long time afterwards, colleagues and I said very little about our experiences in the Battle of the Bogside. Some fellow Red Cross members disapproved of our involvement; indeed, one of our number received a threatening letter. Our silence, though, was not motivated by fear: we hoped that by not 'telling tales' we would preserve the public's confidence and trust in our organisation. This we seemed to achieve as our services, all over the city, continued without interruption.

Welcome to a Strange Land

Pauline Samuelson

LIVING AS I DO NEAR STANSTED AIRPORT, I have witnessed the arrival of two very different groups of people seeking safety in the United Kingdom. The first group consisted of 21,000 Ugandan Asians, who were summarily expelled from their country in October 1972. British passport-holders were given just a few hours to pack their belongings and leave the country. They flew into Britain over a period of seven weeks, arriving on a variety of airlines and always at dead of night to avoid interfering with the airspace of scheduled flights. The second group consisted of Vietnamese Boat People, who had made their own decision to risk their lives on the open seas.

Stansted in 1972 was no more than a collection of Nissen huts, with a small terminal and a two-storey administration building. Its chief asset was a long runway built by the US Air Force in the 1940s. Plans for the Ugandan airlift began when the administration building was converted to a reception centre for both officials and voluntary organisations to work in.

First on the scene was the WRVS with its tea-urns, sandwiches and mountains of old clothes. St John and the Red Cross were given a joint office and regarded by the authorities as one organisation.

Volunteer groups multiplied in numbers during the first 72 hours (before the arrival of the planes), with around 30 assorted and very individual groups making up the throng of hopeful helpers. All the volunteers, totalling some hundreds, considered their presence essential – although what jobs they would do, nobody knew. No single person seemed to be in charge. In fact, 'authority' confined itself strictly to immigration and documentation matters. For some time everyone milled about finding their bearings and speculating on the chance of order emerging out of so much chaos.

St John and the Red Cross settled down to discuss rotas, report books and how we were going to share our skills. We canvassed hard for extra space and coaxed our way through church groups, ethnic support groups and militant students. We successfully gained an extra room for medical treatments and another for a mother and baby nursery. Then we waited for the first plane's arrival.

When the airlift began, at 4 o'clock in the morning, it was raining. Sad, plane-weary bundles of humanity descended the aircraft steps blinking in the strong lights of the runway. Many were either very old or mothers clutching young children. All seemed to register shock and despair as they splashed through the puddles in their colourful, warm-weather clothes towards the reception centre.

We did our best for them during the long hours it took officialdom to go through its protracted procedures. Dawn brought excitement for some lucky ones, with the comfort of family reunions and the start of a new life. For most, however, the next stage was a long coach ride to one of the hastily set-up government reception camps, where more support would be offered by the local Red Cross. The patient, dejected silence of these families said it all. Here were people who one moment had had comfortable lives and control of their destiny, and the next moment were catapulted into a strange environment with nothing familiar to hang on to.

By contrast, the Boat People who flew into Stansted in 1976 were on a high. The plane carried 300 of those who had been shipwrecked and rescued by a British frigate. They had circled the world and had been flying for many days, but they had achieved their goal.

Long before the aircraft was due at midnight, Vietnamese relatives began congregating at the airport. Some had musical instruments to play the plane down, while others had bunches of flowers and banners of welcome. The excitement was palpable and infectious. Everyone waiting for touchdown held their breath. The doors opened and the cheering began. The motley band blared forth into the night and we, the Red Cross, wiped a few tears from our eyes.

There were two stretcher cases – one of exhaustion and the other the result of the shipwreck and hypothermia. To our horror, we also had seven children with measles. Authority in the shape of the District Medical Officer stepped forward: the children would have to go to the local hospital. The Red Cross countered that if they did, the mothers would have to go too. A friendly tussle ensued, but British common sense prevailed. It was agreed to allow the children to reach their London destination before being isolated.

The coach journey to London was an experience never to be forgotten. Once

French was established as the common language, the travellers kept up a volley of questions: pointing to Walthamstow Town Hall, was that Buckingham Palace at last? Driving down Baker Street, did Sherlock Holmes really live there? Passing St Mary's Hospital, Paddington, had Alexander Fleming actually discovered penicillin there?

A Chinese meal awaited our arrival in the disused Kensington Church Street army barracks at 5 o'clock in the morning and we all ate hungrily. Then we escorted our Boat People to their beds. Volunteers from the British Refugee Council had spent the day attaching posies of flowers to bars of lavender soap and placed one on each pillow. There were stars in the eyes of each and every recipient as we bade our farewells and headed back to Stansted.

FALKLANDS PILGRIMAGE

Helen Watson

Helen Watson began her Red Cross service as a VAD in Oxfordshire in the 1950s. She subsequently took a post as a Service Hospitals' welfare officer before moving to London and a career in the International and Youth departments at BRCS headquarters.

TWELVE MONTHS AFTER THE Falkland Islands Conflict of 1982 the British Government kept its promise to take the next of kin and other family members to visit the graves of those who had died in the South Atlantic. Grieving relatives thus had the chance to remember and mourn their loved ones at special services held in the military cemetery and to see the sites where their relatives had fallen.

I was privileged to be one of the 70 escorts who travelled with the 700 people who made this sad pilgrimage. The escorts comprised military personnel, representatives of the Soldiers', Sailors', Airmen's Families Association (SSAFA), people from the War Graves Commission, Service Hospitals' Welfare Officers from the Joint Committee of St John and the Red Cross, and artists from the world of stage and screen.

The journey took us by air to Uruguay and then by sea to the Falklands. We paused at each place where a ship had been sunk so that everyone could remember the servicemen and civilians who had lost their lives at sea.

A lot of organisation went into making the trip as comfortable as possible for the bereaved families. The St John and Red Cross Service Hospitals' Welfare Officers ran a crèche for the youngest children so that they would not be too upset by the mourning and sorrowful atmosphere. This also allowed young mothers a chance to share their feelings with others on the journey, and it gave some of the escorts opportunities to offer one-to-one counselling. In this capacity we found ourselves listening to parents, wives, teenagers and even grandparents, all of whom were struggling to come to terms with the loss of a son, husband, father or grandchild.

Throughout the journey the families did their best to help each other, which made the pilgrimage an extraordinary experience for the escorts. Our role was to offer support to those who needed extra help, and this we did with regular group meetings, lots of tissues at the ready and plenty of hugging for those who wanted it. Adolescents seemed to be particularly shattered by their grief, and we also gave extra attention to parents who were drifting apart because of the loss they had suffered.

Harrowing as this pilgrimage was for the bereaved, it nevertheless marked the beginning of a healing process which helped many of them to accept their loss and start facing the future. Attending the special services and seeing the graves and memorials so lovingly tended certainly left its mark on all of us who were there as escorts.

I am grateful that I was given the chance of helping such courageous people, while at the same time serving the Red Cross in its traditional role of supporting the humanitarian needs of the armed services.

ZEEBRUGGE – A PERSONAL EXPERIENCE

Sue Roberton

A police officer during the 1960s, Sue Roberton joined the Red Cross as County Welfare Officer for Kent in 1986. She later gave valuable service as Senior Service Hospitals' Welfare Officer at the Military Hospital, Woolwich, during the Gulf War. She has now returned to the Kent County Constabulary.

My LIFE CHANGED FOREVER after the evening of Friday, 6 March 1987, when the cross-Channel ferry, *Herald of Free Enterprise*, capsized as it left Zeebrugge harbour in Belgium. Of the 600 on board, 155 passengers and 38 crew died. This tragedy had a profound effect on the lives of those who survived, the families and friends of the deceased, and those, like me, who became caught up in the aftermath.

My husband and younger daughter were both born on 6 March, and as the 7 p.m. ferry left port in Zeebrugge, we were celebrating their birthdays at a local restaurant. I went to bed sublimely happy.

Early the next morning I was woken by a telephone call from Lisa Allen, the Red Cross Welfare Officer in Dover. She told me of the tragedy and how relatives of the crew and passengers were arriving at Dover in vast numbers. They were congregating in three places: the headquarters of Townsend Thoreson (owners of the ferry and now part of the P & O shipping line), the company's ticket office and the Eastern Dock. We decided that Lisa would call out all members of Dover Centre Red Cross and base teams of them where relatives were situated. We were not sure what we would do, but we were going to help in whatever way we could.

The situation at Dover was one of total chaos. Families desperate for news of loved ones had hurried there from all parts of the country, with no thought for their own needs. Some arrived without their regular medication for heart conditions and suchlike, while others had neglected to bring nappies and milk for their babies. For the first few hours our Red Cross volunteers were totally immersed in providing all the practical needs, as well as the 'emotional first aid' of listening, caring and waiting with families.

Some people travelled to Zeebrugge to look for their loved ones in hotels, hospitals and, sadly, in the mortuary. Others were accommodated in local hotels around Dover. The Red Cross was asked to send teams to each hotel to give support and wait for news from Belgium.

Volunteers from other centres around the country were drafted in to help Dover, and rotas were organised so that none of them were exposed to too much for too long. We are often accused of being an uncaring and materialistic society, but I was astounded at the overwhelming offers of help that came from every quarter.

Early on Monday, 9 March, while at one of the Dover hotels, I received a call from Townsend Thoreson asking if the Red Cross could help meet survivors and families arriving back from Zeebrugge. By this time only 60 bodies had been removed from the stricken *Herald*, although there were believed to be over 100 more trapped on board. Rescue work, however, was impeded by deteriorating weather. Meanwhile, survivors were keen to get back to Britain; a few returned by ferry, but most were flown back to their destinations all over the country.

It was at this time that the branch network of the British Red Cross proved invaluable. Suddenly the national fabric of the Society showed a glimmer of its immense potential. The Red Cross was asked if it could meet and transport survivors and their families arriving back in this country from Belgium. Townsend Thoreson agreed to supply resources, which included an incident centre set up at their headquarters, together with desks, telephones and all the food and drink we needed. For the next month volunteers coordinated transport and escorts all over the country from this centre. Drawing on my police experience, I established an incident log, which recorded everything that happened during that period.

Volunteers met survivors and families arriving back in Britain at many airports, including Manston (Ramsgate), Gatwick, Exeter and Manchester. They also arranged for others to be flown out to Zeebrugge to assist with identification procedures, and for some families to sail past the trapped *Herald* and throw flowers on to the water.

Survivors told terrible stories of what had happened when the ship sank. One woman had seen her husband disappear, a woman in a wheelchair sliding away, and children lost. Then everything went pitch black in the icy water.

Inter-agency liaison was extremely important, and within the first days, at the request of the Belgian Red Cross, I travelled to Zeebrugge to meet them and other agencies. Derek Chapman, from British Red Cross National Headquarters, travelled with me for the first planned meeting. I was to meet Dany De Beukeleur from the Belgian Red Cross, former colleagues of mine from the Kent police force and, most importantly, Barbara Townsend, a Red Cross Service Hospitals' Welfare Officer based in Germany who had been working in Zeebrugge following the disaster.

The vital task of coordination at the incident centre in Dover was entrusted to Jinny Lumsden, our Deputy Director in Kent. Meanwhile, volunteers continued working diligently and showed how teamwork pays off.

After the first bodies were repatriated and the survivors taken home, yet more planning had to be done. The ship was still submerged in the water with over 100 bodies on board, and we knew that once they were recovered, more urgent work would be required.

It was five weeks before the ship was eventually safe to board again. It had been like a second disaster waiting to happen. A team of Red Cross volunteers from Kent came out to join me for this second phase. Lisa Allen and I shared a room in the Novotel at Bruges, where a lot of families were accommodated. The remaining members of the team shared a hotel with the mortuary team. I spent a lot of time at meetings and with the families while waiting for the first bodies to be recovered.

I have never before witnessed, or ever wish to again, such emotions as I saw in Zeebrugge at that time. It was so distressing to see families waiting for news of loved ones whom they knew to be dead. All they wanted was to collect the body and go home.

The delay in salvage operations gave us time to plan what role our team should take when the ship was righted. When the time came, we worked in several ways: alongside volunteer drivers of the British Army meeting families on arrival in Belgium; in hotels with the Belgian Red Cross and Kent social workers; and in the hospital mortuary alongside the local Red Cross, Belgian and Kent police officers, padres from the army and other ministers of the Church. Team members often accompanied survivors or families to identify or see loved ones in mortuaries at the St Jan Hospital in Bruges. Emotions were high. After the salvage operation, another 130 bodies were removed from the *Herald*.

Like so many in times of crisis, we learnt to survive by mutual support and team spirit. I have never felt so close to people or so woefully inadequate. The team worked tirelessly for a week, supporting and caring for the bereaved. It was often into the early hours of the morning before families would go to bed; the fear of being alone was prevalent.

Eventually we travelled back to Dover, but our work did not stop there. At a memorial service at Canterbury Cathedral we offered support to relatives, and later it was necessary to attend inquests on all the deceased.

Not long after the Zeebrugge disaster Kent was struck again, this time by a bomb explosion in the barracks at Deal. Once again, Red Cross help was required.

I am sure that there was a once-popular belief that Red Cross members were stored in cupboards with stretchers and bandages, the cupboard doors bearing the inscription 'Open in case of war'. In fact, the British Red Cross is a national organisation, locally run, supported unstintingly by an army of skilful members devoted to the welfare of their fellow human beings. The experience of Zeebrugge showed me how readily members can adapt their skills to deal with matters of such magnitude and gravity. These skills are not locked away in cupboards – they are practised in the everyday life of our members.

Pan Am Flight
No. 103

Dr Alastair Cameron, MBE

Alastair Cameron was Director of the Dumfriesshire Red Cross Branch at the time of the Lockerbie disaster in 1988. Previously he had been the Branch's Medical Officer for many years.

THE DAY WAS ENDING PREDICTABLY, for the shortest day of the year. Since early afternoon, there had been a thick, wet mist shrouding the little town of Lockerbie. Christmas preparations were well advanced and twinkling trees had been sending out their message all day.

At 7.04 p.m. there was a terrifyingly loud noise of a jet aircraft, obviously in desperate trouble, followed by a massive explosion which sent a pillar of fire and smoke hundreds of feet into the air. The worst aircraft disaster in the history of the United Kingdom had occurred.

Hyperactivity, which is the natural response to a shocking occurrence, immediately gripped everyone. Some people rushed to help in the stricken parts of the town, some to assure themselves of the safety of friends and relatives. My abiding memory of that time was of droves of people, on foot, hurrying in the dark, in fearful anticipation. The emergency services and voluntary groups were hurriedly marshalling forces, and there was a consuming curiosity to find out what exactly had happened.

In the next 12 hours it was discovered that a large aircraft had disintegrated in the air. Debris had been scattered over the town, with concentrations in two main areas, and in the environs, extending for many miles. Indeed, documents from the plane were found in the North Sea, over 70 miles from the scene.

In the areas where the concentrations had been noted, there were large numbers of bodies, but many more were found as far as four miles from the town. Ten houses were on fire, and more had been destroyed by huge portions of the aircraft falling on them. Water mains were fractured and electricity was cut off in these areas of the town.

During that night an army of helpers and officials descended on Lockerbie: Police, Fire, Ambulance, Army, Local Authority personnel and hosts of other voluntary organisations, including the Search and Rescue Dogs' Association (SARDA) and the Radio Amateurs' Emergency Network (RAYNET). Many of these volunteers were strangers to the area, and it took some time to realise that local Red Cross members, with their knowledge of the district, had a vital part to play.

Lockerbie Academy, which could accommodate 1,000 pupils during term-time, became the centre of all operations. By 7 a.m. next morning the dining hall was crammed to capacity with all manner of personnel, breakfasting while awaiting the dawn. When asked if anything was required, a group in one corner said, 'Dog food.' It was only then that the dogs were seen, lying quietly at their handlers' feet in the great press of people. These were search and rescue dogs, who had an invaluable part to play. In a matter of minutes the Red Cross representative had an ample supply of food for them, using his local knowledge for the mission.

Another request came from a professor of forensic pathology, who asked for 24-hour first aid cover while he performed almost 500 post-mortem examinations. The Dumfriesshire Branch was able to meet his request. Then, on Christmas morning, there was a sudden call for new combs and toothbrushes; these were required for taking samples from the hair and teeth of the deceased. Again, Red Cross local knowledge could solve this tricky problem.

Part of the Red Cross remit is to support the needs of military and emergency personnel, so when the Branch perceived some gaps it immediately took steps to remedy them. It was obvious that soldiers and police were just as liable to suffer stress from the harrowing nature of their work as were the general public, so Red Cross members gave them a chance to talk and unwind while enjoying their hot rolls and coffee at the first aid posts.

Among those least equipped to cope with stress are army bandsmen, who have no arms training and are used as stretcher bearers in times of armed conflict. At Lockerbie they were employed in moving bodies in the mortuary. One young man, given the task of carrying children's bodies, was so distraught when one disintegrated that he was unable to continue. A Red Cross member spent considerable time helping him to adjust to this distressing experience.

For six weeks the Red Cross was on daily duty, often for long hours. Uniformed members did duty in the maximum security area of the control centre with patience and remarkable good humour. On one occasion I was returning home after one more tiring day, when I was accosted by a weary police sergeant whose remarks I will long remember: 'I just wanted to say, I always thought that the Red Cross was a bit of a joke, but I will never forget all that your people have done here in the last six weeks . . . I never thought it was possible.'

Many books have been written about the Lockerbie disaster, but very few by those who were actually in the mud and darkness of that tragic and never-to-be-forgotten night of 21 December 1988.

THE RED CROSS TODAY

RED CROSS GOES TO THE SEASIDE

Sir Fred Pontin

Sir Fred Pontin is the founder and Life President of the Pontin holiday company, established in 1946, and Pontinental Holiday Villages, which operate abroad. He is an Honorary Vice President of the Dorset Branch of the Red Cross.

LOOKING THROUGH SOME PRESS CUTTINGS the other day, I came across an article with the caption 'Also at Blackpool – but having a different holiday'. It referred to the then prime minister, Edward Heath, having a swim in the sea, alongside another swimmer who had no legs. Behind that caption lies part of my life story of which I am especially proud – Pontin's Red Cross Holidays. The article gives an idea of what these holidays for disabled and elderly people were like 35 years ago, when I first formed my partnership with the Red Cross.

The partnership began through a chance meeting I had in 1960 with Norah Branigan, Director of the Dorset Red Cross. Norah told me about a holiday camp she had been running for several years for disabled people in a disused children's home lent to her by the local authority. Her worry was that the demand for places at the camp was outgrowing her limited space. What did I think about the idea of the Red Cross using some of my chalet accommodation in Weymouth for the camp? My answer was an immediate yes. Pontin's offered Miss Branigan the Riviera Chalet Hotel at half the normal rate for the special weeks of the camp.

The venture was a great success, so the Red Cross National Headquarters suggested that Red Cross Holidays be extended to other Pontin's centres around the country. After much preparation, the Blackpool centre opened for business in the autumn of 1970, followed by the Pakefield Holiday Centre at Lowestoft two years later.

Today, as in those early days, special guests are looked after by Red Cross doctors, trained nurses and volunteers. Over the years some helpers have become real gluttons for punishment, returning season after season. They give up their own holidays and even take cuts in pay in order to help during the special weeks when the Red Cross holidays are held. Gradually, the guest list has grown as the holidays have developed, and now includes people from all over the UK. In 1992 this was widened even further when the northern camp, now at Morecambe, welcomed its first young guests from the Kurdish community in London, and their first visitors from the Royal Star and Garter Home for ex-servicemen and women.

In all the years that I was Chairman and Managing Director of Pontin's Holidays – and, indeed, for several years after I stepped down – the holidays were free, except for a small charge made by the Red Cross for transport and administration. Today, Holiday Club Pontin's makes a modest charge to guests, but in order to offset as much of the cost as possible, the management makes a collection from the general public at all the other Pontin Centres during the season. The resulting cheque is presented each year with due ceremony during the week of the Red Cross Holiday at Morecambe.

When reflecting on my happy involvement with these holidays, I wondered how things had progressed since the 1970s, so I asked the two people who best remember those early days: Nanette Bryce, who has been in charge of the thousand or so guests and helpers at Blackpool and Morecambe almost since the beginning, and Ann Wayre, who has been the Red Cross administrator for the holiday at Lowestoft since its inception. They both reminded me of some of the teething troubles when the holidays were launched – too many wheelchairs and not enough pushers; not enough information about the medical conditions of some of the guests; the spartan nature of the chalets (no heating or carpets) compared to the comfort of the present day. Nanette and Ann also recall that there were precious few telephones in the camps for either guests or organisers; no specially designed coaches for disabled people; no computers to make form-filling easier; and no walkie-talkie radios, which now save so much energy and shoe leather. Much indeed has changed since 1970!

The spirit of the Red Cross Pontin's Holidays, however, never changes. Come rain or shine, the guests, the volunteer helpers and the staff at the centres all make each season's holiday a special week to remember. To join in the fun and to witness the courage of many of the guests is to experience something unforgettable. Whether it is the talent shows, with many a competitor having to be supported at the microphone, judging the competition for the best-dressed wheelchair, or cheering the canoeing that takes place in the swimming pool, the laughter is always there and the enjoyment is contagious.

I am proud to have played a part in enabling these holidays to give such pleasure, and can only be thankful for that chance meeting so many years ago with the Dorset Red Cross.

THE FARNBOROUGH AIR SHOW

Elizabeth Balfour, OBE

A distinguished past Director of the Hampshire Branch from 1946 to 1991, Elizabeth Balfour is now an Honorary Vice President of the Hampshire Red Cross.

HAMPSHIRE RED CROSS INVOLVEMENT at this huge, biennial air show started from the smallest beginnings and has grown into the sophisticated exercise we run today.

World War II was over and the Branch headquarters had moved from its wartime premises into permanent headquarters at Winchester. Normal nursing and first aid duties had been resumed and the Branch was actively engaged in developing its new welfare services in the community. In 1948 we were suddenly asked to provide all the first aid facilities for the public at the Farnborough Air Show, which was moving to its present site at the Royal Aircraft Establishment. We were to be responsible to the senior medical officer of the Establishment, working closely with the county ambulance, police and fire service.

The first thing we had to do was to plan how many first aid posts, doctors, nurses, trained first aiders and ambulances we should need. We then had to decide on what equipment was necessary, and as there were no telephones or mobile radios linking our headquarters with the first aid posts, we had to devise a way of communicating with each other across the airfield using senior boy cadets as messengers. Lastly, plans had to be made for feeding our teams each day and drawing up rotas of volunteers.

For the first year we had three tents as first aid posts and 149 volunteers formed the rota for four days. After each show, all services were reviewed and further planning adjusted to cover developments. This policy proved its worth when disaster struck in 1952 and Farnborough had its first major accident: part of a plane fell into a crowd of spectators.

When the accident occurred, the flying display had already started and all Red Cross members were prepared for the afternoon's duties. Our head-quarters was fully staffed and we had six doctors on call, with a trained nurse in charge of each first aid post. Everyone immediately went into our planned action for a major incident, and first aiders from outlying posts were quickly on the scene where people had been injured. Our vans, which were doing the rounds with tea for the first aiders, were emptied of food and filled with extra stretchers and blankets.

Red Cross ambulances joined the county ambulance service in swiftly dispatching the severely injured to hospitals, while those suffering from minor injuries and shock were treated at first aid posts on the airfield. The teamwork and training proved invaluable during the incident, and the stamina of the volunteers was remarkable. The next day many of the same members were back again at their posts – in dreadful weather – having had only a few hours' sleep since the drama of the day before. Thanks to our National Headquarters in London, our stocks of blankets, stretchers and other equipment were replenished in the early hours of the morning and we were ready for the show as usual when it began at 9.00 a.m.

As the show increased in size and importance, our responsibilities and services grew considerably. The show was gradually extended to cover eight days and included trade tents, a vast exhibition area and static air displays. Red Cross tents were replaced by Portakabins, and electricity and radio made communications far easier for everyone.

Minor casualties continued to be dealt with at each first aid post, but anything more serious was transferred by ambulance to the Red Cross 'hospital' compound for further treatment, or transfer to a general hospital. Casualties came in all sizes; there were wasp stings, blisters, burns, cuts and bruises, eye problems, faints, fractures, heart attacks, strokes and the occasional appendicitis. There were drug addicts and drunkards. There was even a request for water for a budgerigar!

Because of the large number of international visitors, the recording of personal details was a major problem as the spelling of names and addresses could be hazardous!

Forty years and 29 shows later (the event was originally annual) the number of volunteers required has risen from 149 to about 800. A few members give up their annual holiday and are billeted locally for the duration, but the majority travel daily from their homes throughout the county, necessitating highly organised transport arrangements.

The Hampshire Branch has a very heavy programme of first aid duties every year, but the Farnborough Exhibition and Air Show is a highlight where all the Branch's membership works together. The skills of nursing, welfare, child care and first aid are all needed, and the teams into which they are organised provide cover for everyone at this exciting and very demanding event.

THE GENTLE TOUCH

Rula Lenska

Actress Rula Lenska has been a good friend to the British Red Cross for many years. She has done much to support fund-raising through television appearances and speaking engagements in Britain, and has visited refugee camps in Eastern Europe. She remembers hearing stories about her family and the Red Cross which go back to her grandfather who, as a Red Cross official, was charged in 1914 with accompanying the Tsarina on a tour of hospitals and camps at the Russian Front. In 1945 her mother, Countess Tyszkiewicz, was rescued by Count Bernadotte of the Swedish Red Cross from Ravensbruck Concentration Camp.

You MAY WONDER WHY I have chosen to write about something which is so far removed from my own personal experience of the Red Cross. The reason is simple: I believe that there is one Red Cross service which deserves to be trumpeted loudly from the rooftops – Therapeutic Beauty Care.

This service is, above all, a practical example of the way the Red Cross not only helps people like my mother during a major crisis in their lives, but also cares for people with everyday problems. It does, however, require some explanation, as at first glance it seems an odd activity to associate with the Red Cross organisation.

Therapeutic Beauty Care was started 30 years ago and is available to any men or women who may need its help in hospitals, hospices, day centres or residential homes. It encompasses hand care, general beauty care, cosmetic camouflage and beauty care techniques for blind people. The benefits of the service can be imagined once you know about them.

Suppose you were badly affected by arthritis and unable to trim your own fingernails. A hand care volunteer could help you to cope. Hand care can also give a great lift to anyone who has been ill for a long time, or has suffered a recent stroke. Hand care training is the first part of Therapeutic Beauty Care and allows new volunteers to give almost immediate practical help to people after only a couple of days' training.

Beauty care, which consists of face and shoulder massage, requires further training. It is another way of giving a morale boost to someone perhaps suffering from a life-threatening illness or long-standing depression. The feeling of well-being that comes from a volunteer's skilled touch can do much to restore a person's sense of contact with the outside world.

The dependence of blind or partially sighted women on others to help with daily make-up must be especially irritating for the independently minded. Therapeutic Beauty Care teaches what is called 'Familiarity Through Touch' – a method of applying make-up by measuring the face with one's fingers. Learned by listening to a cassette tape and having the assistance of a helper, this technique can give blind or partially sighted people the confidence to apply make-up for themselves.

The fourth part of the Therapeutic Beauty Care Service, and that which demands the greatest skill, is Cosmetic Camouflage. People who need this care are referred to the Red Cross by hospital consultants from a number of specialities.

Among the conditions treated are birthmarks and scars, burn disfigurements such as those sustained by soldiers in the Falklands War (when both Hand Care and Cosmetic Camouflage were used) and a skin cancer called Karposi's Sarcoma, which affects some people with AIDS. Camouflage is also useful in such skin conditions as vitiligo, which is a loss of pigment in the skin. This last condition can affect all races, but is particularly distressing to black and Asian people when it affects the face and makes a marked contrast in skin colour.

In many cases the Cosmetic Camouflage Service helps people to deal with blemishes or disfigurements which, if left un-camouflaged, provoke unwanted stares and hurtful comments from the general public. As one experienced volunteer told me, 'People can often feel quite isolated or rejected on the basis of their appearance. By learning simple cosmetic camouflage techniques, they can draw considerable psychological benefit from their new persona. . . . After all, what may seem like a minimal problem to one observer, can matter a great deal to another individual.'

People want to be judged by their whole selves, not just by their appearance.

The Therapeutic Beauty Care Service is all about making people feel better about themselves. May I also add that this service gives as much satisfaction to the Red Cross volunteers who carry it out as it does to those who benefit from its gentle touch.

HOME FROM HOSPITAL SCHEME

A Grateful Customer

I AM A 59-YEAR-OLD-DIVORCEE who, until recently, worked on an oil-rig in the North Sea. One day I suffered chest pains and was rushed by helicopter to the hospital in Norwich. During various tests the doctors discovered that I have long-term health problems which mean that I can't return to my usual employment. Life suddenly seems very gloomy.

The medical social worker came to see me today and tried to help me organise my life by discussing aspects of it which have to change. For one thing, I know I can't continue living in my flat which is up several flights of stairs. Arrangements will have to be made with the council to exchange it for one on the ground floor because I'm too breathless to climb. The move will be difficult because there's so much I can no longer do. I hope something can be arranged about that.

Good news today – the consultant says I can go home when the discharge has been sorted out. The social worker asked me if there is anyone to help me when I get home and if I have any food in the cupboards, but as I came straight from the rig, there's little likelihood of that. I've been told that the social worker will come back and discuss help from the Red Cross. I haven't a clue what that is, but let's hope it works.

Later the same day: Red Cross Home from Hospital sounds like a good idea, that's if the volunteers turn up . . . I know I shouldn't be pessimistic but this uncertainty gets you down.

Next day: The woman who organises the Red Cross volunteers came to see me and has given me the name of a man who is going to shop for me when I go home tomorrow. His name is Harry and he is going to phone first to get a shopping list.

Returning home: The shopping has been done but the flat seems cold and uninviting after the hospital. The social worker thinks I might be able to get a pension now that I can no longer work. I'm moving next week and another man from the Red Cross is coming to help me shift my few pieces of furniture.

The next week: It's great to know there's somebody to give you a hand. The move went well but I'm still short of a few things like curtains and a cooker that works. In the meantime, I'm having meals on wheels delivered. Harry has phoned twice this week to check I have everything I need.

Third week: Two pairs of curtains and a carpet have arrived today and Harry was around to help me fit them after he had shopped. The Red Cross has also put me in touch with a local charitable trust which has given me enough money to buy a secondhand cooker. Harry's taking me to choose one tomorrow. Life's looking up.

Next year: My doctor says I have to go into hospital again . . . the Red Cross has already helped by taking me to hospital for tests, staying with me while they're done and then bringing me home and making me a cup of tea. Very welcome it was too. The tests have been really unpleasant this time.

Between them, the social worker and the Red Cross Home from Hospital Scheme have been really helpful and I can look forward to having help when I come out of hospital next time. I wonder if it will be Harry visiting then. How many other people don't know about the Red Cross? I'm not sure what I would have done without them . . .

ACTIVENTURE HOLIDAYS

Brian Peck

Y OU WOULD IMAGINE THAT SUCH ACTIVITIES as abseiling, orienteering, canoeing and 'nights in the forest' are confined to extremely fit people. You would be wrong. What is unusual about the holiday camp that I am going to tell you about is that it is specially organised for children and young people who may be fit but who definitely have special needs as well.

My own 11-year-old son, Simon, who is autistic, has now been on three summer Activenture holidays. While my wife and I thought it would be good to send Simon on his own special holiday, we were at first very apprehensive about leaving him, particularly as he needs constant supervision to keep him out of danger. We need not have worried. The high ratio of dedicated carers to children is very reassuring.

Almost every county Branch of the Red Cross runs camps each summer for disabled youngsters and children with special needs. The outstanding feature of these camps is that the Youth Members of the Red Cross are the hosts and carers, and it is this feature that gives these holidays their special appeal. Each Youth Member is responsible for one guest during the entire week. This means being a mate in everything they do, from helping them as they get up in the morning to supporting them in all their activities during the day and sleeping next to them at night.

The guests range in age from 7 to 18 and have a wide range of disabilities and illnesses. In some cases the holidays provide inner-city children with a rare opportunity to visit the country. In most cases these holidays give parents a break which they can enjoy knowing that their youngster is in safe hands.

Hindleap Warren is a purpose-built activity centre owned by the London Federation of Boys' Clubs and situated in 300 acres of the Ashdown Forest. The Sussex Red Cross raises the funds each year to cover seven separate holiday weeks for their invited guests at Christmas, Easter and in the summer. Everyone in the camp is encouraged to take part in all activities under the direction of adult Red Cross leaders and the permanent qualified camp instructors.

Many disabled young people, normally confined to wheelchairs, experience a terrific sense of achievement from, say, climbing to the top of a 20-foot scramble net or reaching the end of a muddy drainpipe in an obstacle race. Every day the surrounding forest echoes to the laughter and shouts from everyone having a wonderful time, and as they emerge each afternoon, dirty with perhaps a bruise or two, they feel triumph in their achievements of the day. I still look in amazement at the photograph of our Simon with safety helmet and harness abseiling down a tree.

For those unable to cope with the more physical activities, there are crafts and gentler sports such as swimming. Activities continue up to bedtime, with discos, karaoke and camp-fire singing, and on fine nights a sleep under the stars is a never-to-be-forgotten experience.

When we have visited Hindleap to deliver or collect Simon, we have been struck by the commitment of everyone in the camp. The Youth Members, in particular, deserve a special mention for their selfless dedication to duty and the marvellous rapport they develop with their young guests. These Youth Members seem to enjoy the experience too and no doubt feel great satisfaction at having given help to others.

Perhaps these Activenture holidays are best summed up by a newly recruited Activenture nurse at the Sussex camp who wrote:

> What I did that week I don't think I will ever forget. I met wonderfully positive-thinking children who were ready to have a go at anything, guests and helpers alike. Group leaders with patience and understanding, who knew when to stand back and when to offer their help and advice. Instructors with seemingly unlimited skills in bringing out the best in people. And then – Di Churchill, the Organiser – always there, always smiling, advising, pushing us to do things to achieve our own goals. And me? Well, I survived. I did some things I never thought I would or could – carried out nursing procedures in some very strange places and thoroughly enjoyed myself. I've already volunteered for next year, and the next, and the next. . . .

THE SIMPLE TRUTH

Jeffrey Archer

As a result of the Simple Truth Campaign in 1991, spearheaded by novelist Jeffrey Archer, thousands of people learned for the first time how the Red Cross and Red Crescent Societies work worldwide, and about the work of the Red Cross in Britain.

In the year of the Gulf War, there was an urgent need to raise funds, particularly for the people of Kurdistan. This single crisis accelerated the British Red Cross fundraising programme dramatically.

Many people who had interested themselves for the first time in the Red Cross as a result of the Simple Truth have continued their regular support. It is this growing band of donors whose generosity enables the Society to meet its worldwide commitment and to fulfil its mission to give skilled care in need and crisis to the people of Britain.

IT WAS EARLY IN APRIL 1991, when I was watching the evening news on television with my family, that I saw a Kurdish grandfather bury his three-day-old grandson on the Iran–Turkish border following his flight from Iraq. As far as the world was concerned, the Gulf War had just ended, but here was a race of people hungry, homeless and terrified.

I phoned John Gray, an old friend at the Red Cross, and asked if anyone was planning a campaign to help the Kurdish refugees, and if not, could I help in any way. I suggested a one-month campaign with some form of entertainment as the highlight, with all the proceeds going to the Red Cross. I realised that such an enterprise could only be guaranteed success if it had the backing of national television, so my next call was to Sir Paul Fox, then head of BBC TV Enterprises. He welcomed the initiative and promised to give it his full

19. First Aid Post in a London underground station, 1941

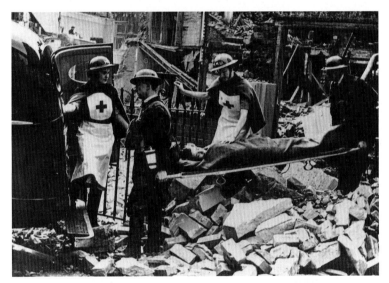

20. Rescuing civilians in the Blitz,
World War II

21. Welfare Officers at work in Italy

22. British Red Cross community work in Malaya, 1950

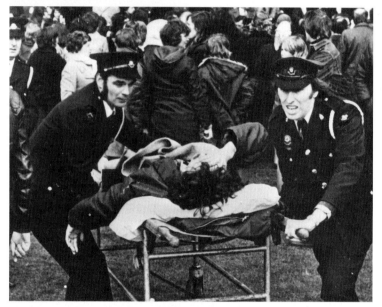

23. First Aid at a football match, 1978

24. Early days of the Pontin's Red Cross holidays

25. Vietnamese refugees in the Red Cross camp, Hong Kong, 1980

26. Famine in the Sudan, 1985

27. Hand treatment being given at a Red Cross Day Centre

28. Learning beauty care technique for blind people

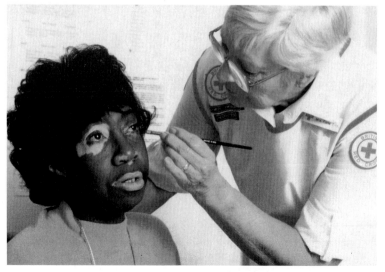

29. Helping some- one to feel better – cosmetic camouflage

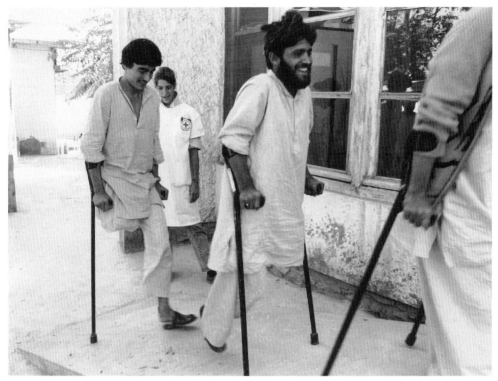

30. Patients in the ICRC hospital Kabul, Afghanistan, 1988

31. Afghan civilian wounded being flown home from Kabul ICRC hospital, 1990

32. Abseiling at the Sussex Activenture Camp

33. Archery practice

34. The obstacle race – leaving the wheelchair behind

35. Kurdish children on the Turkish–Iraqi border, 1991

36. Nigel Havers in Bosnia, 1993

37 & 38. The International Committee of the Red Cross distributing food convoys in Goma, Zaire to refugees from Rwanda, 1994

backing, but warned that it would have to be talent-led and recommended that I should contact impresario Harvey Goldsmith. Harvey, it turned out, had considerable experience of putting on such events, although he had never before been asked to mount such an effort at a month's notice. What was to follow was an experience I will never forget.

The campaign took its name, 'The Simple Truth', from a song by Chris de Burgh, who not only gave his services free on the night of the concert, but also agreed to donate the proceeds from the sale of the record.

An office was set up in my home in London and a team installed. The campaign was to last for one month from 25 April to 25 May, the central focus of the month being the concert on Sunday, 12 May in Wembley Stadium. Everyone involved cleared their diaries and worked long into the nights in order to create what was to be an unforgettable event.

The British Red Cross, supported by their Chairman, the Countess of Limerick, and their Director General, Mike Whitlam, enthusiastically backed the campaign. Contact was then made with other Red Cross Societies around the world to ensure that they would fundraise on the back of the concert, which would be transmitted all over the world.

Supported by the three party leaders and several sporting and entertainment stars, the 'Give a Fiver' campaign was launched. The Prime Minister, John Major, started by pledging a sum of £10,000,000 and encouraged ambassadors to lobby their own governments to give money to the campaign.

The evening of the concert, thanks to Harvey Goldsmith, was a tremendous success. HRH the Princess of Wales attended, as did all three leaders of the political parties. Stars such as MC Hammer, Tom Jones, Snap, the Gypsy Kings, Peter Gabriel, Sting, Beverley Craven and, of course, Chris de Burgh performed live or via satellite, giving their services free.

The great British public responded as generously as ever by raising more than £3,000,000 in individual and corporate gifts to add to our Government's pledge. Other governments and overseas contributions added another £43,000,000, and together with the fundraising which took place on the night of the concert the total raised amounted to a staggering £57 million.

The money spent by the Red Cross over the following months did much to alleviate the suffering in Kurdistan. Trucks, medicines, food, tents and clothing were airlifted to the area, and other UK aid agencies, such as Oxfam, Christian Aid and Save the Children, also benefited from the proceeds of Simple Truth.

As the winter of 1991 set in, I visited Kurdistan with the Red Cross to see how the supplies were helping the thousands of unfortunate people in those desolate mountains. I was given a tremendous welcome. I am fortunate to have many Kurdish friends, and today, with the conflict continuing, I am still working to help them achieve the security and safety they deserve in their own country.

The world of the Red Cross faces new problems every day. The Simple Truth was an example of the Society's ability to move quickly whenever and wherever a crisis occurs. I always wanted the money raised from the campaign to go to an organisation with the experience and integrity to ensure that everyone's donation would be well spent and well administered. I could not have chosen a more responsible organisation, which is why I am delighted to continue supporting the Red Cross in its significant and important 125th year.

THE INTERNATIONAL
RED CROSS

Partnership and Cooperation in Aid

The Rt. Hon Baroness Chalker of Wallasey P. C.

Minister for Overseas Development

W HEN IT COMES TO HELPING beleaguered countries, all non-government organisations (NGOs) want to 'stand alone'. They feel the need to distance themselves not only from the government of their home countries but also the government of the country receiving assistance. It is too easy, for example, in the former Yugoslavia for outside governments, NGOs or the Red Cross to be thought to be siding with one party in the conflict. All NGOs, particularly the Red Cross, need to be seen as impartial and neutral. Supplies of food aid and medical items should be provided to the areas of highest need in humanitarian terms, not to the areas that are most vociferous or to those with stronger political links.

One of the most important jobs of the Overseas Development Administration is to identify these areas of need with the cooperation of the aid agencies and other governments. Then we try to work in partnership with these agencies and governments to deliver the aid.

The Overseas Development Administration (ODA), the aid wing of the Foreign and Commonwealth Office, is responsible for managing Britain's official aid programme. In 1992/93 humanitarian aid accounted for 14 per cent of the department's total expenditure. Most of the department's budget of nearly £2 billion, however, concentrates on longer-term development. The largest part is spent on inter-governmental aid or channelled through the international aid organisations of the United Nations and the European Union.

The ODA recognises very well the vital role of voluntary bodies like the British Red Cross. In fact, it gives financial support and works in partnership with over 100 British NGOs. In recent years the funding for NGOs has increased significantly in recognition of their often unique ability to provide effective aid at the grass roots level, not least for victims of humanitarian disasters. Over half the grants to independent aid agencies and voluntary bodies, which in 1994 totalled over £147 million, was spent on humanitarian aid.

The ODA's Disaster Unit provides a vital round-the-clock link between British aid agencies and the international aid community on overseas disasters. In 1993 the Disaster Unit responded to more than 90 overseas emergencies, several of them in cooperation with the British Red Cross, which holds a stock of emergency supplies on behalf of the unit. It is this sort of cooperation which has ensured that Britain's aid programme functions effectively whether in the form of immediate crisis relief, short-term rehabilitation or long-term restructuring.

The immediate crisis relief work has for many years been carefully handled by the Red Cross, the United Nations and other major international and bilateral agencies. We are anxious to encourage the continuing efforts of these agencies to improve cooperation and coordination in the face of ever-changing new emergencies.

At the other end of the spectrum, a great deal of theoretical and practical effort has been put into longer-term restructuring. In the past there have been too many examples where coordination in this sector has been actively ignored to the point where cooperation turns into competition.

The sector concerned with short-term rehabilitation fits in the middle. It means not only a partnership of aid agencies and governments, but also a heavy reliance on cooperation with immediate relief projects and longer-term development programmes, a process widely called the 'relief development continuum'.

Past examples of poor cooperation are not difficult to find, although I am encouraged to think they are becoming fewer. For example, the inhabitants of Kerala, southwest India, faced a fairly simple problem. The extensive fishing communities rely heavily on wood from mango trees for the manufacture of their boats, but the supply of these trees has been dwindling rapidly. No fewer than seven major agencies tackled the problem and came up with a wide range of different projects and solutions, from the introduction of a plywood boat to a deep-water trawler.

Among the 'solutions' were some that caused difficulties of their own. For instance, the cost of owning and running a trawler would have been well beyond the means of local fishermen. The biggest problem, however, was the lack of cooperation, or partnership, between governments and aid agencies. This rose to a point where, having spent a great deal of time and money on their own ideas, they were reluctant even to acknowledge the value of someone else's project. The result was a mixture of various vessels, all being promoted both locally and nationally, which did little to support the immediate needs of the local people.

The ODA recognised the need for cooperation between agencies, NGOs and governments and within international aid organisations when it became a major sponsor of the United Nations Department of Humanitarian Affairs (DHA), which was established in April 1992. Although still in its early stages, the DHA has already given a new impetus to cooperation between agencies, which, it is hoped, will lead to scarce aid resources being used more efficiently.

In crisis situations the partnership between aid agencies is also of paramount importance. A prime example of partnership was provided by the first camps for displaced people in Somalia in 1992 where the Red Cross and the Save the Children Fund worked side by side. The Red Cross provided medical care and basic food, while Save the Children concentrated on supplementary feeding and health care for children.

Since becoming Minister for Overseas Development, I have come to realise that the importance of cooperation and partnership is a hallmark of good Red Cross practice in the Movement at all levels. A number of examples stand out over the last few years. First, and most important, is the partnership between the Red Cross and Red Crescent National Societies and the International Red Cross and Red Crescent institutions in Geneva, which are themselves heavily supported by National Societies such as the British Red Cross. It is often forgotten that the skills, expertise and practical knowledge of the staff of indigenous voluntary agencies such as local Red Cross/Red Crescent and those of the affected population are very valuable commodities for the immediate relief and continuing rehabilitation of a conflict or disaster zone.

In 1993 the Somali Red Crescent Society was presented with the Red Cross Prize for Peace and Humanity by Her Majesty The Queen. This award recognised the outstanding contribution made by the Somali people towards the enormous humanitarian effort in their country.

In Afghanistan the two major hospitals operating in Kabul are now entirely staffed by Afghani people, ranging from surgeons to nursing auxiliaries. The Red Cross Movement, which still operates extensively in the country, only needs to provide medical support and training for these hospitals which operate on up to 300 wounded a day.

I am convinced that partnership and cooperation between all organisations involved in aid is essential. It is a major aspect to be considered in future relief, rehabilitation and development projects. The role of the International Red Cross and Red Crescent Movement in this picture is vital.

SUDAN DIARY

David Elloway

An active member of the Gloucestershire Red Cross, David Elloway is an Ambulance Officer by profession. He trained as an international field delegate in 1975 and has carried out missions for the Red Cross in Ethiopia, Pakistan and St Vincent. These excerpts from his diary recall the early days of his six-month mission to the Sudan.

November 19th, 1984 – Cheltenham

The phone rang. It was the Red Cross enquiring whether I was available for a mission to Sudan. Many calls later, and after Margaret and I talked about me doing another Red Cross mission abroad, we agreed that it would have to be done.

My chief and my colleagues in the Ambulance Service once again came up trumps by agreeing to cover my work in my absence.

November 21st

I left home with a tearful farewell. Once again I was leaving the comparative sanctuary of England for the 'Lord only knows what'. Whatever else, I was certain it would be hot, dirty and the people would be in very poor shape. It was ever thus.

I was still signing contracts, drawing medical kits, travellers cheques and so on at Red Cross HQ in London just an hour before my departure to Heathrow.

One of my regrets at going on this mission was the fact that I would miss Christmas with my family. The loneliness was compounded even further when the taxi taking me to the airport drove past some Christmas trees already lit up. But the time for regret was over – I was on my way.

November 22nd – Geneva

I reported to the League of Red Cross Societies [now the International Federation of Red Cross and Red Crescent Societies] this morning, and was told that my Scandinavian colleagues had not yet arrived.

Later in the day the others arrived. Briefing started immediately and continued all day. More contracts, luggage, freight papers and seemingly a thousand and one things to do.

At dinner that evening we got to know more about each other: Leif Fischer, from Denmark, an army officer; Leif Sandberg, from Norway, a mining engineer; Elin Merinalo, from Finland, a nurse/nutritionist; and François Piguet, the Swiss team leader, who is a journalist/teacher.

November 23rd

Yet more briefings, interviews, an endless barrage of information; quite exhausting.

By late afternoon we were on our way, three taxis packed with luggage and equipment.

November 24th – Khartoum

02.30 and Africa is very near. My apprehension about the next six months is high now; the mission is bound to be fraught with difficulties and possibly some dangers as well.

After the aircraft had landed and the door opened, a furnace blast of hot, moist air seared its way in. Within five minutes I was soaked. We were met by a member of the Sudanese Red Crescent Society (SRCS) who helped sort out our papers. It took two hours to complete the formalities, and it was just getting light when I got to bed at the Arac Hotel.

About five hours later we were off to more briefings. The chief delegate of the League of Red Cross and Red Crescent Societies met us at their HQ.

An early night for an early start tomorrow.

November 25th

3.30 Khartoum airport. We arrived, but the Sudanair 737 has not, and will not today. We had the joy of being recalled to the airport twice more today.

November 26th

The whole day spent in Khartoum waiting. It is no good getting mad about it – this is Africa, I have seen it all before. In the early hours a DC10 arrived with flour from Holland.

November 27th

05.00 sees us airborne and peeling away from the runway with a pilot who thought he had a fighter plane – I was glad eventually to land in Port Sudan.

We were met by the Red Sea Hills Branch of SRCS. More meetings, more introductions, more information and note-taking. The rest of the day thus occupied.

The night in Africa is very sudden, there is little or no dusk, just the enveloping velvet darkness and the startling contrast of the bright stars. Magic.

November 28th – Port Sudan

The SRCS is anxious to see the Beja nation retain its cultural independence, and the area of our concern is from Port Sudan south almost to Kassala.

We had news of a some 20,000 Bejas in camps along the road to Kassala. Our immediate concern is to start surveying along this road but it has to be done quickly.

Trying to locate transport – buying trucks takes weeks, and renting is next to impossible. It is by no means certain we can get fuel. To be first into this kind of disaster is hard. Tempers fray and no one seems to grasp the urgency of the situation.

November 29th

We left Port Sudan for the first villages.

After driving south, through Sinkat, reached Tahamiam, a large village straddling the railway line. We pulled into the camp and the real impact of the mission started right there. Emaciated, lethargic people everywhere. Children lying in their own waste, sightless eyes glazed over, death the only outcome. I had seen it before, but it still was not easy. My colleague had never seen it and wept unashamedly in a most distressed way. He was unable to talk for several hours.

We moved flour and sugar from our store 19 miles away at Haiya junction. We were to return to the camp many times as our pick-up could only carry 10 bags of flour.

Dr Ali, the district medical officer, told us that his hospital compound in the town of Haiya was overflowing and the population had doubled due to the knowledge that there was a relief camp in Haiya. He had four adult deaths and three sibling deaths before 09.00 this day. Marasmus was the main concern, this being the stage of starvation that makes recovery a protracted affair.

No time to stay, three hours after leaving Haiya, arrived in Derudeb to collect our trucks and Dutch flour and sugar.

The camp at Derudeb holds 10,000 Beja refugees. They had no food, so an immediate ration was made from the back of the first truck.

The town has three good wells giving sweet water. I do wonder how long they will last with an additional 10,000 people.

There are two camps, one medical and one relief. Dr Ali is in charge. He has next to no medicines; even so, he has kept mortality rate within reasonable limits. He is a fine young man. I was destined to work well with him.

The rest of the food from our trucks was unloaded into a storehouse that I managed to hire.

As we were pulling out of Derudeb heading back for Haiya, the sun was already going down.

03.00 saw us stagger into Port Sudan.

November 30th

Fischer returned from Haiya with the news that they have managed to hire a store-house in the town.

Spent the next day preparing to move down-country permanently.

December 3rd – Haiya

We made distributions of food in Tahamiam and Haija. We are concentrating on supplying the two hospitals. It is planned that the first feeding station will be in Tahamiam.

Tim Foster of OXFAM arrived with 120 tins of high-energy biscuits. Tim left the distribution to us as he was on his way through to the south.

What I find in this emergency is the total cooperation between all the agencies at work in Sudan; it's very gratifying.

December 8th – Aderoat

I have worked in many places for the Red Cross and witnessed terrible things but none as poor as this.

We pulled into Aderoat to find people even poorer than in Derudeb. It was absolutely obscene. Human beings so emaciated that they are almost transparent. Clawlike hands plucked at me as I passed. Several of the children being wrapped ready for burial. I could feel vomit surging in my throat.

December 9th – Haiya

I woke up at 04.00 with a very positive attitude today. No more people were to die, at least not because we might weaken, that is. And if anyone stood in our way, then God or Allah help them because we would not.

December 14th

Dr Ali worked with us through the day. He has two assistants helping him and nothing to work with. If ever he felt despair, he managed to hide it. I could see the graveyard has grown since our last visit. I could have wept when he told me of his hopes of a bright future for these people. He was exhausted, but we were not and we vowed that he would never battle with his problems alone again. To my sincere belief we kept that vow.

December 23rd

We had been ordered to Port Sudan for Christmas to meet our team leader's wife. But we are going to have our own Christmas dinner this evening alone. We are pretty close together and we don't want to share any time with anyone else tonight.

My reflections this evening are that we have given water, food, medicine and, above all, hope. We have dispensed from the whole Red Cross world all these things, and the cost is the loneliness that we and our families feel.

I think the price is about right.

A WORLDWIDE MISSION

The Countess of Limerick, CBE

Lady Limerick is Chairman of Council, British Red Cross Society and a Vice President of the International Federation of the Red Cross and Red Crescent Societies.

IN OCTOBER 1993 THE British Red Cross Society was honoured to host for the first time in almost 50 years the Statutory Meetings of the International Red Cross and Red Crescent Movement. Some 600 delegates assembled in Birmingham to decide the policy of the Federation and to debate the issues confronting the Movement.

Her Majesty The Queen, Patron and President of the British Red Cross, was warmly applauded when she addressed the Council of Delegates.

> It is, to say the least, encouraging that the International Red Cross and Red Crescent Movement, always the rock on which the world's efforts to give help and comfort to our fellow human beings is founded, is still growing in size and scope.
>
> You are, of course, uniquely qualified, as the world's largest humanitarian organisation, to provide this life-saving help and comfort. The protection, medical and other assistance, and tracing services of the International Committee, and the relief coordinated by the Federation are vital for the survival of countless men, women and children in all continents.
>
> But what, perhaps, is less well recognised is the untiring work of the National Societies in caring for the daily demands of their own populations: for the sick, the injured, for disabled people, the old, for refugees and for children.

Within this Movement, you have no truck with that depressing and cynical phrase 'compassion fatigue': on the contrary, the human and material resources you devote to the relief of hardship grows greater each year.

This is especially admirable in view of recent instances where dedicated and courageous members of the Movement have lost their lives in the course of duty. I pay tribute to them, and I deplore the disregard for the Geneva Conventions which brought about their death.

I call today on all involved in armed conflict to recognise the neutrality, impartiality and independence of the International Red Cross and Red Crescent Movement. The sanctity of your emblems, and the freedom for those engaged in your work to do so without challenge or fear, must be respected.

The Movement, second only to the UN in its worldwide membership, comprises three operational components: the International Committee of the Red Cross (ICRC), founded in 1863, which has a mandate to protect and assist the victims of armed conflict; National Red Cross or Red Crescent Societies which assist in all kinds of emergency and provide health and social welfare services in their countries; and the International Federation of Red Cross and Red Crescent Societies, founded in 1919, whose secretariat coordinates international relief following natural disasters and assists National Society development.

The components are united by the Movement's humanitarian mission to protect life and human dignity, to relieve suffering and to promote health and social welfare. Their actions are guided by the Movement's fundamental principles, of which the most important are neutrality, impartiality and independence.

It is a sombre reflection of man's inhumanity to man that armed conflict has been a recurrent feature over the past 125 years, and that in the past decade wars have become increasingly frequent, lengthy and cruel. Whereas in World War I civilians accounted for less than 15 per cent of casualties, by the 1990s this figure was nearly 90 per cent in most conflicts. Even when hostilities have ceased, havoc, death and mutilation of civilians continue for decades after: from the 100 million or more anti-personnel mines which lie unmarked on or in the ground in more than 62 countries.

The collapse of political structures and the cycle of conflict, ecological destruction, famine and mass population displacement have contributed to the increasing numbers of people affected by disasters – up from 100 million in 1980 to almost 300 million in the 1990s. Those who suffer most in disasters are socially and economically vulnerable persons, the poor, the elderly, women with children and people with disabilities. That is why the policy of the Federation and National Societies is to focus on disaster prevention through the development of basic services to help the most vulnerable groups in all communities.

International Committee of the Red Cross

The ICRC is a private independent institution whose governing body of Swiss nationals are co-opted to enhance its autonomy and speed of response. (Its international designation applies to its activities, not to its composition.) The secretariat in Geneva coordinates the work of expatriate delegates and locally recruited staff in more than 60 countries. As a specifically neutral intermediary in armed conflicts, it is mandated by the Geneva Conventions and Protocols to protect and assist the victims of international wars (see Appendices). In civil wars it is authorised to offer its services to the government and to the leaders of opposing armed groups. Neither party is obliged to accept and there may be many months of negotiation before the ICRC can reach the victims on all sides. Frequently, other organisations, by assisting one party only, are not able to enter areas controlled by another, and the ICRC may be the only organisation to succeed in reaching all victims.

The ICRC is also entitled by its statutes to take humanitarian initiatives to protect those in situations not covered by the Geneva Conventions or Protocols, such as internal tension or disturbances. (The ICRC first made visits to so-called 'political' detainees in Russia in 1918 after the 1917 Revolution.) Since World War II, it has visited over half a million political detainees in almost 100 countries, many in South America, South Africa and parts of the Far East.

The ICRC is active in the world today on an unprecedented scale. It has five areas of activity carried out with the help of National Societies, relating to protection, medical aid, relief, tracing and dissemination work. In some circumstances it has joint operations with the Federation. In 1993 its activities reached a record high, with field expenditure totalling £370 million, 143,610 detainees visited in 47 countries and over 4 million Red Cross message exchanges between members of families separated by conflict or disturbances.

The International Federation of Red Cross and Red Crescent Societies

The Federation has a membership of 162 National Societies with a further 23 in formation and an annual operating budget of £10 billion, and over 125 million members worldwide.

The Federation's multinational secretariat staff in Geneva launched 31 emergency relief appeals in 1993. Population movements, mainly generated by conflicts, were the biggest single cause of aid appeals, of which the largest were for refugees and displaced persons in the former Yugoslavia, medico-social assistance to the newly independent states of the former Soviet Union and rehabilitation in Somalia. At any one time, 300 expatriate delegates are working 65 countries on behalf of the Federation and in support of the efforts of thousands of National Society Red Cross and Red Crescent volunteers.

British Red Cross Society

Since its foundation in 1870, the British Red Cross has made frequent reviews of its role and activities, taking into account its founding objectives and both local and international events. In accordance with its 1990 mission 'to give skilled and impartial care to people in need and crisis in their own homes and in the community, at home and abroad, in peace and war', during the 1990–91 Gulf War, Service Hospitals' Welfare Officers were dispatched to field hospitals in the conflict zone, while Red Cross and St John volunteers at home were mobilised to give nursing and welfare assistance to the medical services of the armed forces and to the NHS in anticipation of large numbers of casualties returning to the UK. In accordance with its principles of neutrality and impartiality, Red Cross assistance was also given to families of British POWs and to families of Iraqis detained in the UK.

In its 125th year, the British Red Cross has a combined Adult and Youth membership of 93,000 volunteers, 286 paid staff at its NHQ and about 1,200 paid staff in its network of 90 Branches in England, Wales, Scotland and Northern Ireland, the Isle of Man and the Channel Islands. The Society has 6 Branches and 3 Committees in overseas territories. The Society's annual income totals some £60 million from all sources.

The five core services which British Red Cross members provide to help the most vulnerable people in time of crisis are:

1) **Emergency Programme** – response to an unexpected or local emergency in support of the statutory services with first aid, transport, escort and comfort for the survivors, bereaved relatives and rescuers. The British Red Cross Disaster Appeal Scheme assists local authorities in launching an immediate appeal. The Society is also designated to distribute European Union grants to disaster victims and their families.

2) **Community Programme** – core services include first aid cover at some 40,000 events annually; escort service for housebound persons needing

to travel; medical and nursing equipment for short-term home use and the Therapeutic Beauty Care and Cosmetic Camouflage Service.

3) **Training Programme** – first aid for Red Cross volunteers, first aiders in the workplace and members of the public. First aid training has been extended to meet the needs of deaf or visually impaired persons, those who speak no English, and occupational groups such as motorists, farmers and oil-rig workers. A babysitters course is a popular innovation for teenagers.

A range of courses on 'managing stress and crisis' help all sorts of people to cope with psychological and emotional trauma.

Other training courses in ambulance aid, nursing, welfare, community care, other care skills and international humanitarian law are also organised.

4) **Youth Programme** – encompasses a wide range of learning and service-giving activities. In 1991 a National Youth Forum was established, which elects three members to the National Council. Youth members are also represented on Branch Committees and at Regional Meetings.

5) **International Programme** – within the UK the International Tracing and Welfare service dealt with 2,678 enquiries in 1993. The number of Red Cross messages received and dispatched more than doubled to 12,835; 60 per cent of these related to the former Yugoslavia and 35 per cent to Somalia.

National Headquarters, on behalf of UNHCR, also deals with family reunion applications. Most recently it coordinated reunions for 2,045 Bosnian evacuees.

Refugees are cared for in three Red Cross centres in the UK. In the year up to February 1994 more than 300 refugees from the former Yugoslavia passed through these centres, and a confidential register of children arriving unaccompanied has been established.

The International Programme (outside the UK) gives relief to victims of conflict and disaster. As well as funding individual programmes, the British Red Cross also supports the operations of the ICRC and the Federation with finance, materials, equipment and expert personnel.

The British Red Cross also places increasing importance on development, helping vulnerable communities to achieve better health, water and sanitation. It also gives institutional support to sister National Societies. The total amount spent on overseas work has risen from about £5 million in 1985 to about £30 million in the 1990s. The money, spent in the form of cash assistance, personnel and goods, was distributed to over 50 countries around the world.

The British Red Cross runs an Overseas Delegates Training Course which is open to members of National Societies and other aid agencies. In mid-1994, nearly 100 delegates were in the field in some 30 countries. The previous year 172 overseas missions were undertaken by British Red Cross staff and delegates.

Dissemination and protection of the Red Cross emblem is a major concern of the British Society. To facilitate this it has established courses on International Humanitarian Law, which are open to academics, health professionals, civil servants, journalists, law students and the general public.

During the 1990s, the horrendous human suffering caused by armed conflict waged with repeated disregard for humanitarian principles or the rules of war has been brought into stark reality in the former Yugoslavia, Somalia, Angola, Rwanda and other strife-torn countries. Indeed, the scale of suffering from both manmade and natural disasters is proof that the International Red Cross and Red Crescent Movement, and the British Red Cross in particular, is needed as much in the 1990s as when it was founded over 125 years ago.

VISIT TO BOSNIA

Henry Jones-Davies

Henry Jones-Davies, now a freelance writer living in west Wales, has lived in Turkey and Saudi Arabia and has travelled widely. He has worked for the World Health Organisation, and as a security consultant, professional hunter, film producer and journalist. He is the author of several books.

IN JANUARY 1994 I FLEW with actor Nigel Havers to the Croatian capital, Zagreb, to help raise funds for the British Red Cross effort to bring relief and comfort to the hundreds of thousands of refugees fleeing the slaughter and persecution in Bosnia. Though the majority of these refugees are Muslims, many are Croat and Catholic. In the crowded camps in and around Zagreb, religion is of little importance. What matters is survival, and hope.

The Croatian authorities provide what assistance they can, but with the prospect of an all-out war in Bosnia-Herzegovina and an economy on a conflict footing, money and personnel are in short supply.

'First aid' for the dispossessed and the traumatised of Bosnia's dirty war is provided by the International Federation of Red Cross and Red Crescent Societies, with our own British Red Cross at the forefront of the effort to alleviate the chaos and dislocation which the refugees, from babes-in-arms to the old, sick and infirm, inevitably suffer.

During a two-day visit, Havers visited five camps of varying size. Some were 'illegal', established without the blessing of the Croatian authorities, holding unregistered refugees, while others were registered with the government as transit camps – in both cases, a refugee's first step to relocation in a friendly country and a new, uncertain, life.

Among the smokestacks of a grim industrial complex on the outskirts of

Zagreb, a former workers' cooperative hall has been turned into an 'illegal' transit camp for Bosnian Muslim refugees. One hundred and fifty refugees of all ages are crammed into five small prefabricated rooms. They share a single lavatory and wash-basin. Washing hangs from makeshift lines in a mud-pooled yard, and rubbish spills from rusted oil-drums in the street outside. The children of the camp are playing here among the puddles and the broken asphalt. The men stand around the fences, sullen and silent in this social and political limbo. To welcome our group, coffee is brewed and a bottle of Bacardi served in eggcups. This is all the refugees have to offer and it is given without hesitation, which is how they expect us to accept.

During the night, as on most nights, a group of 10 to 15 wanderers from Bosnia will arrive at the camp. They will have relatives or friends here, and word passes quickly. Room will be made for them, no one will be turned away. Thus the camps, and the refugee problem, continue to grow.

With a current total of more than 530,000 registered refugees, a population of 4.7 million Croatians and no end to conflict in sight, Red Cross officials reckon that the problem will still exist in five years' time, with up to 2 million homeless and stateless refugees searching for any sort of future.

Typically, a family arriving at an 'illegal' camp will have been subjected to a stiff dose of, at best, bullying and, at worst, the trauma of witnessing close family members executed, raped or tortured. The 'fortunate' survivors will have signed away the rights to their homes, packed a suitcase or two with warm clothes and a few treasured possessions, and obtained transit documents at exorbitant rates from contemporary Harry Limes capitalising on the chaos of this war. The last of the family's foreign currency savings buys a one-way trip out by truck or coach.

The only refuge for Bosnian Muslims is Croatia: to enter Serbia would mean extermination. Once on the move, the first shock comes with the discovery that the hugely expensive transit documents are forged. The second comes later, when refugees find that without proper documentation they can't get out of Croatia – even if there is a cousin in Sydney or Ottawa or Copenhagen willing to take them in. Negotiations with foreign legations in Zagreb take on a hopeless, Kafkaesque air. This is where the Red Cross comes in.

The relief effort of the British Red Cross in former Yugoslavia is impressive indeed, with more than 32 expatriate delegates at work full time, and a back-up team of local assistants and social workers of the highest calibre. The 1994 programme includes a food distribution plan for Central Bosnia, with half a million individual food parcels to be distributed in the region over a one-month period, an infant-care parcel programme, projects to provide emergency shelter, a water support project to supply 10 per cent of the total requirement for the besieged city of Sarajevo, a haemodialysis programme for renal failure patients, and a project to provide a total of 20,000 emergency stoves both for cooking and space heating. All this to offer immediate relief in a pitiless, and this year, very early, winter.

From its headquarters in Zagreb, the Red Cross team organises a turnkey relief operation with efficiency, determination, good humour and, all too frequently, with courage. The list of British delegates reveals a wide spectrum of skills and tasks, from field nurses, nutritionists and engineers, to mechanics and HGV drivers, all working with skill and professionalism to bring the means of survival, and the comfort and hope to give people the will to live through the horror of it all.

The Red Cross, too, provides a vital service simply monitoring the camps, their inmates and their growing numbers. Where huge numbers of displaced persons are spread over such a wide area, in many cases over many different countries and continents, the Red Cross operates an efficient tracing service to track down lost relations and friends. In situations throughout the world where people have little to hope for, this service provides that hope, and real results, as photographs of family reunions show only too poignantly.

During the visit we became aware of the political tightrope the organisation has to tread. Often, government representatives try to score propaganda points off the Red Cross's activities, and staff are specifically trained to sidestep such situations as skilfully as possible. Havers was aware of this when an enthusiastic young reporter from one of Croatia's leading daily newspapers asked him publicly to condemn Serbian atrocities after talking to a group of refugees. His measured response drew a sigh of relief from the Red Cross representatives present. As Geoffrey Dennis, British Red Cross International Director, told me, the organisation has to operate in all sectors of a war without displaying any political, ethnic or ideological affiliation, and it is only too easy to become embroiled in the media point-scoring of propagandists.

Havers was invited by the Red Cross as part of its overall fund-raising campaign to take part in a live link-up from Zagreb with GMTV in London, and he gave his services without hesitation. It was refreshing to see an actor getting down to the business of helping others, instead of the customary and unseemly habit of some members of his profession of meddling in contentious and often sleazy issues, and this was appreciated by both the senior officers of the Red Cross and by many refugees who recognised him from television. His humour and natural compassion coaxed smiles from despairing faces in many dismal surroundings.

For Havers, the most poignant moment of the visit, after a series of distressing interviews, was when a group of young children from a camp at Sisak, a frequently shelled town to the south of Zagreb, put on a performance of a classic children's play about the love of a simple shepherd for a princess – opposed by a jealous, sword-waving warlord – for the residents of an old people's home. Each of these children, a mixed group of Bosnian Muslims and Croats, had first-hand experience of horror, with parents tortured or killed, homes looted and burned. They were withdrawn and uncommunicative when they first arrived at Sisak, but Irena Barisic, a social worker with the Red Cross, has transformed them into a lively and enthusiastic troupe of players.

Despite the seriously grim surroundings of their camp, a former barrack for factory workers, these children had found something to help them go on living, not just to survive, but to achieve, on a personal and collective level, something which lifted them high above the horror, the boredom and the depression, something of which to be proud.

The efforts of the Red Cross often get sidelined by more glamorous stories, of UN convoys, of last-minute diplomatic deals over negotiating tables in the smart hotels of Europe's smarter cities, by details of the fearsome technology of war, or the polished soundbites of the politicians.

There is not much that an individual, outraged by the suffering in former Yugoslavia, can do, perhaps, just two-and-a-bit jet hours away from the slaughter in Bosnia. But putting one's hand in one's pocket for the Red Cross effort really can do a great deal, if not to influence the outcome of the conflict, then certainly to alleviate the starvation, suffering and dislocation. By the way, despite the warlord, the shepherd in the children's story won his princess.

'ANXIOUS FOR NEWS'

Nigel Havers

Actor Nigel Havers first went to the former Yugoslavia in October 1992 in order to help the British Red Cross get publicity and urgently needed donations for its work in the region. He was very moved by what he saw on this trip and promised to return. A year later, the British Red Cross took him back to Croatia to find out what had happened to the refugees still living there and to see how Red Cross operations had expanded to deal with the increased humanitarian demand. Nigel was joined on this second trip by GMTV and freelance journalist Henry Jones-Davies. He was particularly impressed by the tracing and message service of the Red Cross, and here is his report.

IN THE WORLD TODAY THERE ARE more than 20 million refugees and something like 23 million people displaced within the borders of their own countries. Conflict and famine produce two of the most frequent causes for whole populations to leave their communities and homes in search of peace and survival.

Red Cross history first records help being given to refugees in 1875, when relief was sent by the International Committee of the Red Cross to the people of Montenegro who were fleeing the fighting in Herzegovina. Now, 120 years later, the Red Cross is still providing relief for the people of Bosnia and Herzegovina, as I have myself witnessed in that war-torn country.

In places like the former Yugoslavia and, indeed, anywhere in the world where there is political upheaval, famine or natural disaster, two humanitarian services in particular can lift the hopes and hearts of desperate families torn apart by circumstances. These are the Tracing and Message Services of the Red Cross. But how do they work and why are they special to the Red Cross? The services are unique because they have the force of the 1949 Geneva Convention and additional Protocols (1974) behind them. They are therefore *mandatory* services, which are carried out by National Red Cross and Red Crescent Societies across the world.

The Message Service relays family messages in crisis situations where normal communications have broken down or – as in prisoner-of-war and refugee camps – where communications don't exist. The Tracing Service performs minor miracles daily in reuniting families who may have lost touch for perhaps half a century due to war, and who may happily be brought together again thanks to the long and painstaking work of an international tracing team.

The services began, like most Red Cross aid, as humanitarian support of the armed forces and soldiers who were made prisoners during the Franco-Prussian War of 1870. A special relief and information bureau was set up in Basle, Switzerland, to provide news for families of relatives who had been taken prisoner. Lists of prisoners were provided by both the French and Prussian authorities.

This service continues today between warring parties and the International Committee of the Red Cross (ICRC) based on either the application of the Geneva Conventions or on the ICRC's right of initiative. In such circumstances, ICRC delegates register prisoners of war (providing security against disappearance) and endeavour to establish a Message Service link between them and their relatives.

Civilian victims of war were included in the 1949 Geneva Convention, and from the early Basle Bureau grew the Central Tracing Agency, which is still the responsibility of the ICRC in Geneva.

The Central Tracing Agency holds over 70 million names, and the International Tracing Service in Germany, managed by the ICRC, holds another 46 million reference cards relating to the 14 million people persecuted by the Nazi regime.

As in some conflicts civilians may account for nearly 90 per cent of victims, a great deal of the Agency's work is with people who have never taken up arms. Indeed, children all too frequently feature in this work as the victims of indiscriminate shelling.

ICRC delegates are sent to all parts of the world, where their sensitive task is to deal with civilian internees, prisoners of war and tracing enquiries in places where impartiality and neutrality are of immense importance. Whereas Geneva and the Central Tracing Agency were in the past the 'home base' for all such work, much of it is now decentralised to ICRC delegations in key areas.

National Societies play a great part in delivering the Tracing and Message

Services, and enquiries to do with tracing are often directly initiated between sister Societies. This is particularly the case after natural disasters, such as the massive 1994 earthquake in Los Angeles, when families in their thousands anxiously enquired about relatives in the affected area.

Confidentiality is always the watchword and no information is ever divulged without permission of the person concerned. Societies like the British Red Cross use their own network of Branches and members for tracing and message purposes. The Tracing Service, in particular, can give an extra lift to the everyday duties of an ordinary member, as enquiries are sometimes made about an individual in their own town or village by a relative living on the other side of the globe. If the tracing enquiry has a happy ending, the feeling of reward is enormous.

Today the British Red Cross traces more than one family per day. I was told about a 16-year-old Eritrean girl who had to flee her home and was brought to England as a servant by a rich Sudanese family. When she contacted the Red Cross, she was frightened of trying to find her family for fear of making trouble for them. She had not seen her parents for seven years and could hardly remember anything of her childhood other than the name of her village. The Tracing Service set to and the happy outcome was an eventual telephone call from the delighted young girl telling the Red Cross that she had just received a letter from her sister in Eritrea.

Sometimes, however, the good news comes too late, as it did for this mother who wrote to the Red Cross in Polish from Byelorussia:

> I have 95 years and I am looking for my son, Adam, born 1918 . . .
> I am living only hoping to see him or to get some news about him. I
> shall wait to the last moment of my life. He was in the Polish Army
> and I am crying for him for 50 years now. Before I die, I want to
> know what happened to him and then I shall be able to die in peace.

The sad news was that Adam himself had died in Hertfordshire in 1981, but after a great deal more work, one of Adam's sons set off for the village in Byelorussia to meet his grandmother, only to find she had died two weeks before his arrival. On a brighter note, Adam's four sons and his mother's 10 great-grandchildren are now all in touch and getting to know each other.

The challenges facing the International Welfare Department of the British Red Cross are enormous and I can only give a general idea of the lifelines they are often able to offer. It is hard to imagine what it must be like to lose a home and family. In the former Yugoslavia I have seen for myself the faces of people scanning the message board pinned up in the town square of Sisak and the excitement when they found their own family name listed. The Tracing and Message Services, like so much else in the Red Cross, seek to alleviate human suffering in the most practical way. I know, because I have seen the joy that long-awaited news can bring.

REBUILDING MY LIFE

Alen Pešić

This is the personal story of how one medical evacuee from the former Yugoslavia is managing to build a new life in Britain after experiencing the devastating effects of civil war in his country.

WHAT DOES THE RED CROSS MEAN to me personally? What I am about to tell you involves an atrocity of war. I want to tell you my story because I owe my life to the Red Cross and I want people in this country to know that.

I was an ordinary citizen of Yugoslavia and then of Bosnia-Herzegovina, living an ordinary life – not active in politics. I was a medical doctor working in a Sarajevo teaching hospital.

The war started on 4 April 1992; at first it was a very local conflict and nobody thought it would spread. Everyone thought common sense would prevail, so no one moved away from their homes or tried to leave the country. After about a month the shelling began in Sarajevo and there were times when I could not leave the hospital and had to stay there for up to eight days at a time. I found sleeping in the hospital and not going home quite tiring, so after a while the hospital devised a shift system where doctors would be on duty for a week or so and then have 10 days off. During a period of time off I decided to take my family out of the dangers of Sarajevo. My parents are retired and had no reason to risk their lives in town, and my younger brother was able to leave with us as well.

We went to a quieter part of Bosnia, to an aunt who had room for my parents and brother. I had a ID pass with my photo on it which would allow me to get back through the barricades to my work. In the early days hospitals were respected and not shelled. But after my 10-day break, I could not get back to

Sarajevo because fighting had broken out in an area between my aunt's house and the city.

It was during the time that I was staying with my aunt that the army began arresting people in a systematic and very brutal fashion. They came to my aunt's house with guns bristling and checked our names. If you had the 'wrong name', that is a non-Serbian name, you were arrested. Imagine all the Joneses and McGregors being arrested in England because they had Welsh or Scottish names! That was how it was – and I was taken off to a detention camp.

To give you some idea of what it was like in this camp, when I arrived there people were being beaten and killed daily. After about three months the International Committee of the Red Cross were finally permitted into the camp. For us this was a sort of liberation. The ICRC gave us some kind of identity cards and insisted on talking to us without two guards being present. They explained to us that the cards were important because they proved our existence. We would now be registered on computers with the ICRC in Geneva, and if we disappeared, the Red Cross would have details that could help to find us. After this happened the killings stopped. People were still beaten, but they were always revived and were not left to die. So you see, the Red Cross saved many lives just by giving us bits of paper.

The next stage was the arrival of an ICRC doctor – I remember him so well. He began treating the most urgent medical cases in the camp.

Gradually, thanks to the media and press, the world began to take notice of these camps. At first those running the camps denied their existence. Then, when they were cornered, they claimed that everyone in the camps was a prisoner of war. (This was absurd, as inmates included women, young boys of 12 and 13 and many old men.) Right, said the Red Cross, if they were prisoners of war, then everyone was entitled to protection under the Geneva Convention and they – the ICRC as custodians of the Geneva Conventions – must see that their terms were carried out. One of these terms is medical treatment for those who need it.

So it was that arrangements were made for 68 of us to leave the camp. Britain, who at that stage had taken fewer people from former Yugoslavia than countries like Germany and Austria, agreed to take all 68 of us.

Up to that point our care had been in the hands of the ICRC. When we arrived in the UK, the British Red Cross took over. We were put into hospital where many of us continued to have treatment for up to six months. The Refugee Council, at that early stage, did not have a section dealing with Bosnia, so much of the work, including such legal questions as what constitutes 'a family', was sorted out by the Red Cross.

Although we found peace and security in Britain, our problems were far from over. So many people were involved with our welfare – the hospital, the social services, Bosnian humanitarian groups – it was quite a muddle at times. Even though I was in a wheelchair suffering severe nerve damage of the legs, I worked as an interpreter because there didn't seem to be many other people who could do the job. I want to tell you that despite all the problems, which most people are really not aware of, the Red Cross achieved a lot for all of us. The Message Service worked miracles considering the difficulties it had to overcome. When there are fierce battles going on and millions of people are leaving their homes and moving from place to place, it is wonderful that families can keep in touch through the Red Cross Message Service.

After some time we were moved into the vacant nurses' home of the hospital. There I stayed until I was fortunate enough to be allocated a ninth-floor flat in a high-rise council block which has a marvellous view of the sea.

I am now slowly recovering from the beri-beri which affects my walking and comes from a vitamin deficiency suffered through my time in the camp. But you don't need legs for what I am doing at the moment. I am studying very hard to get back to my profession. I need British qualifications to be able to get a job here as a paediatrician, and I am lucky in that the English language is not a problem for me.

I miss my family and my beloved country, of course. But I am gradually building a new life in Britain – the country that gave me asylum when I so desperately needed it.

A VOTE OF THANKS

Squadron Leader
Robert Ankerson

Robert Ankerson and his pilot had to abandon their Tornado bomber aircraft over Iraq on 24 January 1991 during the Gulf War, and both were taken prisoner. Unlike some of his captured colleagues who were forced to appear on television, Ankerson was kept incommunicado and his wife had no news of him for six weeks, until the day before his release.

The following extract is taken from his speech at a Red Cross gala evening held at the Royal Albert Hall in 1992.

EARLY ON 5 MARCH 1991 IN BAGHDAD several Iraqi officers came into my cell to tell me I was to be released. The moment of my freedom and that of the other POWs was about 10.30 that day when I walked past numerous Iraqi soldiers into the entrance of the Novotel in Baghdad. After walking through the crowded foyer, we were led into a room where we were greeted by at least six people wearing smiling faces and Red Cross badges. After about half an hour, we were escorted in small groups by a Red Cross official up several floors. You may be able to appreciate our apprehension as we were still deep in Iraq with not an Allied soldier in sight. We were assured by our escort, a petite lady from the Red Cross, that we were now safe. To us it appeared we were still far from safe and I asked who was protecting us. She replied immediately that *she* was – all five feet one of her! When I asked who was protecting her, she pointed to the Red Cross badge she was wearing and said that was providing the protection. It had worked for the last 10 years and she was certain it would work now. Thankfully, it did. I don't think any other organisation could achieve this role as effectively.

However, the Red Cross don't always get it right first time. I hope they were not offended when, instead of using the individual rooms that they had provided for us, we felt happier, after up to seven weeks of virtual solitary confinement, to move in together, which in some cases meant four to a room.

After being delayed overnight in Baghdad and having feasted on copious quantities of Swiss chocolate provided by one of your directors from Geneva, we flew out of Iraq on 6 March. As we neared the border in the Red Cross aircraft, I had the opportunity to talk directly to my wife on a telephone link through Geneva, but that was only on the second attempt as she hung up on the first connection when she heard a German voice and thought it was the press. Fortunately, the operator in Geneva tried again and this time I got through.

All the British POWs went to Akrotiri in Cyprus where, as well as having the Service's medical care, we were again fortunate to have two Red Cross ladies to help us. They sorted out clothes, shoes, watches and other odds and ends for us and were also there for a chat when needed. I know the men in the organisation make an equal contribution to the work of the Red Cross, but I have to say that those ladies both in Baghdad and Cyprus added something to our welcome to freedom.

These short interludes are inadequate illustrations of the effect you all have on the lives of thousands. For myself, and the countless others who will continue to receive your help, thank you.

APPENDICES

APPENDIX 1

Profile of the International Red Cross and Red Crescent Movement

International Committee of the Red Cross (ICRC)

Foundation – 1863.

Status – Private, independent, Swiss institution.

Role – Acts as a neutral intermediary in humanitarian matters during international armed conflicts, civil wars and internal strife. Its role during armed conflicts is defined in the four Geneva Conventions of 1949 and their Additional Protocols of 1977.

Aim – Provides protection and assistance to: both military and civilian victims, prisoners of war, civilian detainees, war wounded, and civilian populations in occupied territory. Also visits political detainees.

Composition of Committee – A maximum of 25 Swiss citizens.

Headquarters – Geneva, Switzerland, with 604 members of staff (1993). Expatriate staff 862; from National Societies 175; local employees 4,800. Staff work in over 60 countries.

Finance – Voluntary contributions from governments, the European Union, National Societies and private donors.

International Federation of Red Cross and Red Crescent Societies

Foundation – 1919.

Purposes – To encourage the creation and development of National Societies throughout the world.

To coordinate international relief for victims of natural disasters.

To care for refugees outside areas of conflict.

To help National Societies with disaster preparedness and long-term development projects for the most vulnerable.

Headquarters – Geneva, Switzerland. Secretariat staff of 250, with 380 expatriate overseas delegates (1993). Staff are working in 65 countries at any one time.

Finance – Annual dues from National Societies and voluntary contributions from the European Union and others for relief and development operations.

National Red Cross and National Red Crescent Societies

Foundation – Each Society has its own foundation date. The British Red Cross Society was founded in 1870.

By 1994 there were more than 160 recognised National Societies.

There are approximately 125 million members of the Movement.

Red Crescent – The red crescent emblem was first used by Turkey during the Russo-Turkish War in 1876.

Turkey, which acceded to the Geneva Convention in 1865, informed the Swiss Federal Council, the custodian of the Convention, that it would henceforth display the sign of the red crescent instead of the red cross. The ICRC regretted that uniformity of the emblem would not be maintained.

At the Diplomatic Conference of 1929, the red crescent emblem was formally recognised. The Conference deemed it necessary to stress the absence of any religious significance.

Recognition – Only one National Society can be recognised in each country.

Societies must fulfil stringent conditions to achieve recognition by the ICRC and obtain Federation membership.

Societies must be recognised by their governments as Voluntary Aid Societies, auxiliary to the public authorities in the humanitarian field.

Membership – Open to all, and services are provided solely on the basis of need.

Wartime functions include: Auxiliary to the medical services of the Armed Forces.

Care for military wounded and sick.

Care for prisoners, refugees, displaced persons and civilian internees.

Ethos – National Societies and other components of the Movement are united by a set of Fundamental Principles (see Appendix 2).

Services – Societies carry out services according to the needs of the respective countries they serve. They include:

Emergency relief

Emergency and disaster preparedness plans

International Tracing and Message Service

Health and social assistance to individuals

Training in auxiliary nursing and first aid

First aid courses for the public

Blood donor support for transfusion services

Youth programmes

Care in epidemics, including HIV/Aids

Community health and social welfare

Education in humanitarian law

Headquarters – Each Society has a National Headquarters, which assists in the management of the Society and its voluntary membership.

Finance – Societies are independent of their governments. Funding of service varies, but generally depends on public contributions, income-generating activities and some government grants.

APPENDIX 2

The Fundamental Principles of the International Red Cross and Red Crescent Movement

Humanity

The International Red Cross and Red Crescent Movement, born of a desire to bring assistance without discrimination to the wounded on the battlefield, endeavours, in its international and national capacity, to prevent and alleviate human suffering wherever it may be found. Its purpose is to protect life and health and to ensure respect for the human being. It promotes mutual understanding, friendship, cooperation and lasting peace amongst all peoples.

Impartiality

It makes no discrimination as to nationality, race, religious beliefs, class or political opinions. It endeavours to relieve the suffering of individuals, being guided solely by their needs, and to give priority to the most urgent cases of distress.

Neutrality

In order to continue to enjoy the confidence of all, the Movement may not take sides in hostilities, or engage at any time in controversies of a political, racial, religious or ideological nature.

Independence

The Movement is independent. The National Societies, while auxiliaries in the humanitarian services of their governments and subject to the laws of their respective countries, must always maintain their autonomy so that they may be able at all times to act in accordance with the principles of the Movement.

Voluntary Service

As a voluntary relief movement, it is not prompted in any manner by desire for gain.

Unity

There can be only one Red Cross or one Red Crescent Society in any one country. It must be open to all. It must carry on its humanitarian work throughout its territory.

Universality

The International Red Cross and Red Crescent Movement, in which all Societies have equal status and share equal responsibilities and duties in helping each other, is worldwide.

APPENDIX 3

The Geneva Conventions

Closely related to the establishment of the Red Cross, the Geneva Conventions are international agreements which, in essence, set out a code of practice relating to the care and protection of war victims. Their main historical development was as follows:

1864   First convention, for the amelioration of the condition of the wounded and sick in armed forces in the field.
1906   Second convention, for the amelioration of the condition of wounded, sick and shipwrecked members of armed forces at sea.
1929   Third convention, relating to the treatment of prisoners of war.
1949   Fourth convention, relating to the protection of civilian persons in time of war.

Additional Protocols, 1977

Protocol I – Relating to the protection of victims of international armed conflicts.
Protocol II – Relating to the protection of victims of non-international armed conflicts.

The three Conventions extending the original Geneva Convention of 1864 were adopted to provide protection for more categories of war victims. There are now four Geneva Conventions, which were adopted by member states in 1949, covering armed forces on land, at sea, prisoners of war and civilians. These treaties have been accepted by virtually every country in the world.

In addition, two new treaties, called Protocols, were drawn up in 1977. These add to and update the 1949 Geneva Conventions, taking into account

190

modern means of warfare and aiming to give greater protection to civilians.

There are no set rules for the names of treaties, which are written agreements between states, governed by international law. The term 'protocol' is, however, often used to describe a treaty which adds to an existing treaty, and it seems that this is why the term was chosen in this instance.

Enforcement of the Geneva Conventions and Protocols is often difficult because, to a great extent, it depends on the state applying those treaties.

APPENDIX 4

The British Red Cross 1995

1995 is a celebration of 125 years of the unique humanitarian activities of the British Red Cross at home and abroad.

This birthday gives a golden opportunity to celebrate the vital role of the British Red Cross in providing neutral and impartial assistance to victims as an integral part of the International Red Cross and Red Crescent Movement; trained and skilled response to disasters and emergencies; community services to care for people in crisis.

1995 is also a time to remember the selfless work of past generations of volunteers and professionals. A major campaign for money and volunteers to meet the ever increasing demands made upon these services has been launched.

As a volunteer organisation, the British Red Cross relies on the commitment and energy of some 90,000 members working across the country, and on the skill and professionalism of those who undertake its work overseas.

Priorities for the 125th Birthday Appeal

Four areas of service have been highlighted for priority in the campaign in Red Cross Branches throughout the United Kingdom during this 125th birthday year. The development of these services will ensure that the standard of care and professionalism for which the British Red Cross is acclaimed can continue with confidence well into the next century.

Emergency Response Teams

There are plans to recruit and train 60 additional Emergency Response Teams, serving over 100 local communities.

First Aid Training

The British Red Cross aims to produce the resources necessary to teach vital life-saving skills to one million people.

Medical Loan

51 new Medical Loan Centres will open providing essential medical equipment to patients on short-term loan.

Home Care Teams

23 Home Care Teams, each bringing help to people with disabilities, will be recruited and trained.

Appendix 5

NHQ
British Red Cross Branch Addresses

England

Avon Branch
Red Cross House
Alma Road Avenue
Bristol BS8 2DX

Bedfordshire Branch
Red Cross County Office
99 Ashburnham Road
Bedford MK40 1EA

Berkshire Branch
48 London Road
Reading RG1 5AR

Buckinghamshire Branch
123 London Road
High Wycombe
Buckinghamshire HP11 1BY

Cambridgeshire Branch
2 Shaftesbury Road
Cambridge CB2 2BW

Cheshire Branch
Red Cross House
20 Bexton Road
Knutsford
Cheshire WA16 0DS

Cleveland Branch
30 Park Road North
Middlesbrough
Cleveland TS1 3LF

Cornwall Branch
Russell House
Lighterage Hill
Newham
Truro TR1 2XR

Cumbria Branch
Woolpack Yard
Kendal
Cumbria LA9 4NG

Derbyshire Branch
Red Cross House
Matlock Green
Matlock
Derbyshire DE4 3EG

Devon Branch
Ermen House
Butts Road
Heavitree
Exeter
Devon EX2 5BD

Dorset Branch
Red Cross County Office
Westminster Road
Wareham
Dorset BH20 4SW

Durham Branch
Flass House
Waddington Street
Durham DH1 4BG

Essex Branch
Red Cross House
200 New London Road
Chelmsford
Essex CM2 9AD

Gloucestershire Branch
Red Cross House
Cainscross
Stroud
Gloucestershire GL5 4JQ

Hampshire Branch
Red Cross House
Weeke
Winchester SO22 5JD

Hereford and Worcester Branch
Red Cross House
Green Hill
London Road
Worcester WR5 2AE

Hertfordshire Branch
Baker Street
Hertford SG13 7HT

Humberside Branch
40 Norwood
Beverley
Humberside HU17 9EW

Isle of Wight Branch
Red Cross House
1 Hunnyhill
Newport
Isle of Wight PO30 5HJ

Kent Branch
Red Cross House
25 College Road
Maidstone ME15 6SX

Lancashire Branch
Red Cross House
316 Blackpool Road
Fulwood
Preston PR2 3AE

Leicestershire Branch
Red Cross House
244 London Road
Leicester LE2 1RN

Lincolnshire Branch
22 London Road
Grantham
Lincolnshire NG31 6EJ

London Branch
28 Worple Road
Wimbledon
London SW19 4EE

Greater Manchester Branch
Red Cross House
439 Lower Broughton Road
Salford M7 9FX

Merseyside Branch
Red Cross House
4 Tuebrook Terrace
346 West Derby Road
Liverpool L13 7HG

West Midlands Branch
34 Blossomfield Road
Solihull
West Midlands B91 1NS

Norfolk Branch
Coronation Road
Norwich NR6 5HD

Northamptonshire Branch
Red Cross House
51 Billing Road
Northampton NN1 5DB

Northumbria Branch
Croft House
Western Avenue
Newcastle upon Tyne NE4 8SR

Nottinghamshire Branch
31 Gregory Street
Lenton
Nottingham NG7 2PA

Oxfordshire Branch
101 Banbury Road
Oxford OX2 6JY

Princess Mary House Branch
Queen Parade
Harrogate
North Yorkshire HG1 5PP

Shropshire Branch
Sutton Lodge
Betton Street
Belle Vue
Shrewsbury
Shropshire SY3 7NY

Somerset Branch
Red Cross House
Livingstone Way
Taunton
Somerset TA2 6BD

Staffordshire Branch
24 St Leonard's Avenue
Stafford ST17 4LU

Suffolk Branch
Red Cross House
Lamdin Road
Bury St Edmunds IP32 6NU

Surrey Branch
Red Cross Headquarters
Woodlands Road
Slyfield Green
Guildford GU1 1RL

Sussex Branch
Sussex Branch Headquarters
3–4 Howard Terrace
Brighton BN1 3TR

Warwickshire Branch
Red Cross House
6 Warwick New Road
Leamington Spa CV32 5JF

Wiltshire Branch
Red Cross House
Semington
Trowbridge
Wiltshire BA14 6JW

North Yorkshire Branch
62 Thirsk Road
Northallerton DL6 1PN

South Yorkshire Branch
53 Clarkegrove Road
Sheffield S10 2NH

West Yorkshire Branch
Beech House
333 Leeds Road
Idle
Bradford BD10 9AB

Wales

Addresses of Branch Headquarters in Wales as at October 1994.

Several Branches are merging and Branch Headquarters addresses may change during 1995. Please contact your local Centre.

Clwyd Branch
Red Cross Headquarters
Victoria Avenue
Prestatyn
Clwyd LL19 9DF

Dyfed Branch
16 Spilman Street
Carmarthen SA31 1JY

Mid Glamorgan Branch
Red Cross House
18 Pentrebach Road
Glyntaff
Pontypridd CF37 4BW

South Glamorgan Branch
The Coach House
St Fagan's Road
Fairwater
Cardiff CF5 3XR

West Glamorgan Branch
42 Sketty Road
Swansea SA2 0LJ

Gwent Branch
35 Stow Park Circle
Newport
Gwent NP9 4HF

Gwynedd Branch
Red Cross House
Oxford Road
Llandudno LL30 1DH

Powys Branch
Powys Branch Headquarters
31 Park Street
Newtown
Powys SY16 1EF

Scotland

Scottish Central Council Branch
Alexandra House
204 Bath Street
Glasgow G2 4HL

Angus Branch
130 East High Street
Forfar
Angus DD8 2ER

Argyll Branch
Tweeddale Street
Oban
Argyll PA34 5DD

Ayrshire & Arran Branch
18 Wellington Square
Ayr KA7 1HA

Berwickshire Branch
25 Market Square
Duns
Berwickshire TD11 3DB

Bute Branch
Cairncraig
56 Crichton Road
Rothesay
Isle of Bute PA20 9JT

Caithness Branch
9 High Street
Thurso
Caithness KW14 8AG

Dumfries & Galloway Branch
Nith Avenue
Dumfries DG1 1EF

Dunbartonshire Branch
116 East Princes Street
Helensburgh G84 7DQ

Dundee Branch
51 Reform Street
Dundee DD1 1SL

East and Midlothian Branch
c/o 62 Great King Street
Edinburgh EH3 6QY

Edinburgh Branch
62 Great King Street
Edinburgh EH3 6QY

Ettrick & Lauderdale Branch
Red Cross Centre
18 High Street
Selkirk TD7 4DD

Fife Branch
Frankfield House
22 Carlyle Road
Kirkcaldy KY1 1DB

Forth Valley Branch
Red Cross House
1 Glebe Avenue
Stirling FK8 2HZ

Glasgow & Renfrewshire Branch
14 Elliot Place
Glasgow G3 8EP

Grampian Branch
Red Cross House
22 Queens Road
Aberdeen AB1 6YT

Inverness-shire Branch
Forbes House
36 Huntly Street
Inverness
IV3 5PR

Lanarkshire Branch
6 Auchingramont Road
Hamilton
Lanarkshire ML3 6JT

Moray Branch
80 South Street
Elgin IV30 1JG

Nairn Branch
Red Cross Centre
5 Queen Street
Nairn IV12 4AA

Orkney Branch
68 Victoria Street
Kirkwall
Orkney KW15 1DN

Perth and Kinross Branch
14 New Row
Perth PH1 5QA

Ross and Cromarty Branch
20 Hill Street
Dingwall
Ross-shire IV15 9JP

Roxburgh Branch
17 High Street
Hawick
Roxburghshire TD9 0EN

Shetland Branch
Old Tolbooth
Commercial Street
Lerwick
Shetland ZE1 0HX

Sutherland Branch
Red Cross Centre
Brora
Sutherland KW9 6NX

Tweeddale Branch
21 Old Town
Peebles EH45 8JF

West Lothian Branch
217 High Street
Linlithgow
West Lothian EH49 7EN

Western Isles Branch
54 Bayhead Street
Stornoway
Isle of Lewis PA87 2DZ

Central Council Branch

Isle of Man Central Council Branch
Red Cross House
Derby Road
Douglas
Isle of Man IM2 3EN

Northern Ireland

**Northern Ireland Central Council
Branch**
87 University Street
Belfast BT7 1HP

Belfast Branch
Top Floor
87 University Street
Belfast BT7 1HP

Down Branch
The Lady Mairi Bury House
20 Hamilton Road
Bangor
Co. Down

Northern Branch
42 Mill Street
Ballymena
Co. Antrim BT43 5AS

Southern Branch
Co-ordinator
Stormhill
Tullyvar Road
Aughnacloy
Co. Tyrone BT69 6BL

Western Branch
Omagh Business Complex
Gortrush Industrial Estate
Omagh
Co. Tyrone BT78 5LS

Channel Islands

Bailiwick of Guernsey Branch
Red Cross House
Rohais
St Peter Port
Guernsey
Channel Islands

Jersey BRCS Committee
The Chairman
La Rigondaine
Grouville
Jersey
Channel Islands JE3 9UU

BRCS Branches and Committees Overseas

Hong Kong Red Cross
Anne Black Building
33 Harcourt Road
Hong Kong

Bermuda Branch
PO Box HM772
Hamilton HM CX

British Virgin Islands Branch
PO Box 178
Road Town
Tortola

Falkland Islands Branch
PO Box 465
Port Stanley

Gibraltar Branch
24 Brittania House
New Marina Bay

Montserrat Branch
PO Box 61
Dagenham
Plymouth

Anguilla Red Cross Committee
c/o Education Department
The Valley
Anguilla
West Indies

Cayman Islands
Red Cross Committee
PO Box 1713
George Town
Grand Cayman
Cayman Islands

Turks and Caicos Islands
Red Cross Committee
Chief Secretary's Office
Government Complex
Pan Am Base
Grand Turk

ACKNOWLEDGEMENTS

The Editor and Publisher gratefully acknowledge the help of the following people and organisations in the preparation of this book:

C.E.A. Baird, Chairman, Jersey Committee of the British Red Cross.
The estate of J.L.A. Cary for permission to quote from *A Memoir of the Bobotes*.
Diana Churchill, Sussex Red Cross Branch.
Mrs Corrigan, Chief Librarian, Jersey Library, Channel Islands.
Lady Winefride Freeman for quoted material on Dunkirk and the East Coast Floods.
Mrs C.M. Hurley for permission to use the poem 'The Red Cross Bloke'.
Maude Jones, CBE, for assistance with historical matters.
Ella Jordan, who gave permission, prior to her death in 1993, to quote from her book *Operation Mercy*, published by Frederick Muller.
Mr Hugh Lenfesty, Archivist, Guernsey Archives, Channel Islands.
Brenda McBryde for kindly allowing the letter from Belsen to be used.
Michael Meyer, Barrister, British Red Cross National Headquarters.
John Murray (Publishers) Ltd for permission to quote from *A Traveller's Prelude* by Freya Stark.
Margaret Poulter, Archivist, British Red Cross, 1985–93.
Leonie Trouteaud, MBE, for assistance with the Guernsey material.
The Hon. Mrs David Verney for permission to use material from Lady Falmouth's diary.
Ethel Viedler for quoted material on the Blitz.
Emily Wood, British Red Cross National Headquarters.

INDEX